To Tom

All the best!

*[signature]*

Happy Birthday
2007

*Gregory Kelser's*

# TALES FROM
# MICHIGAN STATE

## GREGORY KELSER
### AND
### STEVE GRINCZEL

### FOREWORDS BY JUD HEATHCOTE
### AND TOM IZZO

SportsPublishingLLC.com

ISBN 10: 1-59670-051-3
ISBN 13: 978-1-59670-051-2

Publishers: Peter L. Bannon and Joseph J. Bannon Sr.
Senior managing editor: Susan M. Moyer
Acquisitions editors: Mike Pearson and John Fishel
Developmental editor: Mark Newton
Art director: K. Jeffrey Higgerson
Cover design: Dustin Hubbart
Interior layout: Heidi Norsen
Photo editor: Erin Linden-Levy

Sports Publishing L.L.C.
804 North Neil Street
Champaign, IL 61820
Phone: 1-877-424-2665
Fax: 217-363-2073
SportsPublishingLLC.com

Printed in the United States of America

Library of Congress Cataloging-in-Publication Data

Kelser, Gregory, 1957-
   [Tales from Michigan State]
   Gregory Kelser's tales from Michigan State / Gregory Kelser and Steve Grinczel ; forewords by Jud Heathcote and Tom Izzo.
      p. cm.
   ISBN-13: 978-1-59670-051-2 (hard cover : alk. paper)
   ISBN-10: 1-59670-051-3 (hard cover : alk. paper)
   1. Michigan State University--Basketball--History. 2. Michigan State Spartans (Basketball team)--History. 3. Kelser, Gregory, 1957- I. Grinczel, Steve. II. Title.

GV885.43.M53K45 2006
796.323'630977427--dc22
                                  2006028398

For my wife, Donna; my mom, Verna;
and my brother, Raymond.
And in loving memory of my dad, Walter Kelser Jr.,
and my grandparents, Alice and Willie Parker,
and Anne and Walter Kelser Sr.
—G. K.


To Joyce, my wife of 26 years, my soul mate and
best friend for 30, and the love of my life forever.
—S. G.

# CONTENTS

# PREFACE

The man knows what he wants in a pancake. Blueberries, for one thing. Not too many, though. Regular maple syrup, and plenty of it. An order of turkey sausage on the side would be nice. Oh, you have grits? I love grits. I'd like some of those too, please. And could I have some sliced tomato? A tall glass of water will be just fine.

It didn't matter what time of the day we met, Greg Kelser—"Gregory" as Jud Heathcote, his former Michigan State basketball coach unfailingly and affectionately calls him—ordered pancakes, which are an appropriate metaphor for what he wanted out of basketball, a career and life. Unpretentious, substantial, sustaining, and on his terms.

Often over mouthfuls of syrup-saturated cake, Greg told his story in the course of more than 40 hours of conversation. The result is *Gregory Kelser's Tales from Michigan State*, which I like to think is more than a collection of war stories former players years removed from their glory days tell each other at reunions or over dinner when passing through town. To be sure, there are plenty of "I remember when . . ." tales in the following pages. But what Greg has chosen to do is put into words something that's part autobiography, part memoir, part history lesson, and part guidebook that coaches and players can look to for inspiration and illustrations of what goes into becoming a champion.

Without question, a major component of Michigan State's run to the 1979 national championship was the wealth of talent that some will say "magically" came together in East Lansing, Michigan, over the course of two seasons. Most of the potential—or as the '79 Spartans would say *P-O-T-E-N-T-I-A-L*—was in place when Earvin Johnson arrived from just up the street in neighboring Lansing to trigger a big bang that still resonates throughout college basketball. Much of it was gathered by former head coach Gus Ganakas and his assistant Vernon Payne, who from the very beginning identified Greg as someone they could build a national championship program around. Greg was an all-around scorer and phenomenal athlete who barely got noticed at Detroit Henry Ford High School. Measured by contemporary standards, however, Greg's ability to fly through the air, dunk, and shoot off the dribble would be coveted not only by today's sophisticated recruiters from coast to coast, but by talent evaluators for decades to come. I once asked Greg if he knew how high he could jump, and he said, "High enough."

Some of MSU's potential came by the way of pure serendipity, as was the case with Jay Vincent and Mike Brkovich. Vincent was Earvin Johnson's crosstown high school rival and embodied athleticism, power, and skill rarely found in a big man. What's more, he chose MSU because he wanted to play close to home. How many communities the size of Lansing produce two players as good as Vincent and Johnson in the same year who wind up on the same college team? The sweet-shooting Brkovich wasn't even recruited. He was discovered while playing pickup basketball at Michigan State's venerable Jenison Field House.

Coaches around the country would love to have one player like Kelser, Johnson, or Vincent, or even one like Ron "Bobo" Charles, who accepted and thrived in a less prominent role for the good of the team. Then there were the so-called glue guys such as Mike Longaker who, prior to becoming a brilliant surgeon, served as the cooling voice of reason in the crucible Heathcote held over intense heat. It was Heathcote, of course, who relentlessly hammered away at Kelser's potential until it was fully realized. The result was an unforgettable leading role in a game that ranks amongst the most significant in college basketball history.

Greg, MSU's first First-Team Academic All-American, told his story eloquently, with amazing clarity and an uncanny recollection of detail. One time, he recalled a sequence of games during which he became Michigan State's all-time scoring leader. Without hesitation, he said he had 39 points to go heading into Iowa, Ohio State, and Indiana, but thought he only got "something like" 13, 11, and 10 points in those games. When I called Paulette Martis at the MSU sports information department to pull out the old box scores and verify Greg's "fuzzy" memory, I about dropped the phone when she said, "13, 11, and 10."

Greg Kelser breathed life back into events that have been buried in his scrapbook for some 25 years while telling the backstory of how the Spartans survived near-disastrous trials and tribulations just to get to "The Game That Changed the Game." Hardly a rehash of well-known events, the story from Greg's point of view strips away some of the hazy film that builds up over time to reveal a rich, warm patina.

Today, Greg is a highly successful broadcaster in Detroit and a much-demanded public speaker. And if you ever run into him at a restaurant, don't be surprised to find him eating blueberry pancakes at four in the afternoon.

—Steve Grinczel
East Lansing, Michigan
May 2006

# FOREWORD

**A**s Gregory's coach for three years and friend for more than 25, I feel honored to play a small part in his book. The first time I ever saw Gregory play was in late April three weeks after I had accepted the Michigan State job. It was during a pick-up game with our returning players and a couple of recruits. Vern Payne, a holdover assistant coach from Gus Ganakas' staff, had been singing Gregory's praises because of his outstanding freshman season. As I watched Gregory play, I was immediately impressed with his athletic ability. He could run like a deer and had tremendous leaping ability. The longer I watched, however, the more I was unimpressed with his shooting, dribbling, and ball-handling.

I called Gregory into my office shortly thereafter and expressed my concern for his total game. To my amazement, he agreed with my evaluation. He said that at Henry Ford High School and during his freshman year at Michigan State he always played in the basket area and knew he had to improve most other aspects of his game to realize his potential.

We talked about summer jobs, and he was adamant that he wanted to work half-days so he could spend the other halves on his game. I realized after that first meeting that Gregory was someone "special." He was intelligent enough to recognize his shortcomings and driven to improve them. This was the beginning of Gregory's dedication to the game of basketball. In all my coaching years there was no one who worked harder than Gregory or put in more hours to become a better player. I would like to take credit for Gregory's improvement each year, but the truth is the credit belongs to him. Gregory made himself a great player.

I'm not going to bore the reader with statistics or repeat anecdotes that are chronicled here by Gregory, but I do have a few favorite "Gregory stories."

The first involves his graduation. Gregory was selected first-team Academic All-America his senior year. This was a great honor for him, the university, and the basketball program. He had planned to complete his degree requirements by attending summer school. However, the Detroit Pistons wanted him in their summer program, so he was unable to attend class. I facetiously kept telling Gregory he was embarrassing the program because when we bragged him up to our recruits they invariably asked, "What did he graduate in?" Then we would have to say, "Oh, Gregory didn't graduate. He's just an Academic All-American."

Gregory felt the pressure and enrolled in classes both spring quarters after his first two seasons with the Pistons. I still remember Gregory coming into the upstairs gym in mid-May with a smile on his face, saying, "Coach, I just turned in my final paper, I'm all done." I said, "That must be an anvil off your back," and he replied, "No, it's you off my back." We both have told that story a number of times through the years, and it never fails to get a chuckle from the audience.

The second occurred prior to our national championship game with Indiana State. NCAA rules mandate that the coach bring two players to the press conference the day before the game. Naturally, I brought Gregory and Earvin Johnson. The format called for all three of us to be available for questions and answers during the formal session, and then we were to split up for one-on-one interviews. I warned both players that there were a number of freelance writers who were searching for anything controversial and that they should be prepared because these writers would try to get negative comments about Larry Bird. The three-person session went very well as I fielded almost all of the questions. I stated that I understood we were favored to win because we had two superstars and a good supporting cast, whereas Indiana State had one superstar and a good supporting cast.

We then broke up for the one-on-one sessions, and I did not see either Gregory or Magic until we got in the car. I said, "How did it go?" and they both started to giggle. "Coach," Magic said, "Do you think I'm as good as Larry Bird, because that's what they kept asking, and I just kept saying, 'I hope I can be half as good as Bird.'" Gregory said, "They kept asking me who was best, Magic or Bird, and I just said 'They are both All-Americans, and I'm honored to play with one and against the other.'" I said that those were good answers, and they both said, "Yeah, but we gave those answers 20 times regardless of the question. They must think we're idiots." They kept laughing until we got back to the hotel.

The third is an inside joke Gregory, Magic, and I have shared over the years. I used to work with Gregory after practice on pivot moves. All the other players would shoot their free throws and then leave, but not Magic. He hated to leave after practice and would watch Gregory and me. One night he said, "Coach, why don't I stand behind Gregory so he can shoot over some defense?" I said fine, but soon Magic insisted that he be on offense so Gregory could work on his defense. Each of them developed a good hook shot although Gregory put it to use in games much more than Magic because he was in the post and Magic was at the guard position.

When Magic was playing for the Los Angeles Lakers, he scored 42 points in Game 6 of the NBA Finals to beat Philadelphia for the championship when Kareem Abdul-Jabbar was out with an injury. Several of those 42 points came on hook shots, and the media quizzed him on where he learned the hook since he didn't shoot them from the guard position. Magic said, "I learned the skyhook from Kareem Abdul-Jabbar." When Magic came home for the summer, I posted him up on that statement. I said, "Magic, you learned that hook shot from working with Gregory." He replied, "Coach, I know that, you know that, and Gregory knows that, but that isn't what they wanted to hear."

I would be remiss if I didn't comment on Gregory's pro career. He was drafted No. 4 in the first round by the Pistons, and the consensus was that he didn't live up to expectations. I will believe until the day I die that if Gregory could have avoided injury, he would have had a long and productive NBA career. He had a number of breakthrough games, but before he could capitalize on them, he would get another nagging injury. Gregory's biggest problem was he played harder and more aggressively than his body could stand. I asked Don Monson, my assistant coach at MSU during Gregory's sophomore and junior seasons, what he remembered most about Gregory Kelser, and he answered, "Always a class act both on and off the floor."

As you read about the games, the alley-oops, the honorary degree, the Hall of Fame, the successful TV career, and all the rest, keep in mind that you are hearing from one of the greatest Spartans of all time—*a real class act!*

—Jud Heathcote
Michigan State Head Basketball Coach 1976–1995

# FOREWORD

I first became personally aware of Gregory Kelser when my Northern Michigan team made the long journey to East Lansing to play Michigan State in December of 1975. I made my first collegiate start against MSU the previous year in Marquette, and this was the return game. Gregory was a very thin but incredibly athletic forward who had a good game against us even though he was playing in only his fifth game as a Spartan freshman. With Terry Furlow and Bob Chapman, Michigan State had a pretty good team that year but only beat us by 16 points. Like anybody would after having played a team like the Spartans, I followed them a lot closer the rest of the season. Two years later, the "magic show" arrived and Gregory started to dominate in his own way.

It just so happened that I attended my first Final Four in 1979, one year after I graduated from Northern Michigan. With Gregory and his high-wire act and Magic Johnson throwing him lobs, I made it a point to learn even more about him, and I was in Salt Lake City when the Spartans beat Larry Bird and Indiana State for the national title. I got to know the real Gregory Kelser, however, when I became a graduate assistant coach under Jud Heathcote at Michigan State. Gregory came around often to visit, play pickup ball, or work out. Then I'd hear Jud talk to everybody we recruited and every player we coached about what Gregory Kelser meant to MSU during his playing days. He was the outstanding student; he was the off-the-court character guy; he was the on-the-court standout. Jud always had high praise for him.

As I became more involved in recruiting as a full-fledged assistant in '86, Greg came back for a lot of football games, and I started to rely on him a little bit. He couldn't do much with recruits, but he was so good with our players and our coaches, and it was special because he was a role model we could point to with great pride.

Once I got the Michigan State head coaching job, he became even more important to me because I knew the only chance I had of luring some big-time players to the program was to somehow form a link to the past. I hired Gus, who recruited Gregory, to bring the guys from the '50s and '60s back into our consciousness, and Gregory of course took care of the '70s. There was a natural bridge between the '57 Michigan

State team that went to the Final Four and Gregory's '79 team that won the national championship and what I was trying to do. I think tradition still plays a very key role for the country's greatest football and basketball programs even in this day and age when it seems like there's a lot more of "What did you do for me today?" At the time, Gregory was our only first-team Academic All-American, so we also played that up. Through his TV career, which involved broadcasting Big Ten games, we got to spend even more time with him.

What I appreciated most about Gregory is that any time I thought it would be great to have him appear at an event—a football game, a reunion game, a meeting, a big recruiting weekend—he'd be back at the drop of a hat. He's one of those guys who just exudes class, and because of that I wanted him around as much as possible. I didn't want to monopolize his time, and yet every time I saw him, he always said, "Whatever I can do, just let me know."

From a coaching standpoint, I don't like Gregory Kelser, I *love* him for how he's treated me and what he's meant to our university, because even though it's been 27 years since he won a national championship, he's been able to maintain his position in the spotlight and his star status. With a lot of guys, you wonder, "How long will it last?" With someone like Magic, it endures because of who he is. Because of what Gregory has been able to do with his life after basketball, he also has sustained the glow. He's everything you could hope for. He's got the academic achievement, the athletic acclaim, and the professional reputation. He is the soul of this program in many ways

—Tom Izzo
Michigan State Head Basketball Coach 1995–present

# ACKNOWLEDGMENTS

**W**ith all due respect to Gregory Kelser's remarkable steel-trap memory, a project such as this involves too many names, facts, figures, dates, and events for one person to remember precisely after 20, 30, and even 40 years. Getting his story as mistake-free as possible couldn't have been accomplished without the access to the Michigan State University Sports Information Department archives granted by associate athletic director for communications John Lewandowski. I thank MSU men's basketball SID Matt Larson, sports information office assistant Paulette Martis, and assistant SID Ben Phleger for their timely and unflaggingly patient assistance. Thank you also to University of Detroit Mercy sports information director Mark Engel and his staff, and Mona Burke at Detroit Henry Ford High School. I must also acknowledge *Detroit Free Press* sportswriter Mick McCabe for setting me straight as only he can, and MSU superfan Scott Jackson for his valuable suggestions. I can't express enough gratitude to Sports Publishing and editor Mark Newton for the unbelievable flexibility and accommodation afforded to me during extremely trying times. I'd like to show my heartfelt appreciation to my sisters—Joanne Brasic, Ruth Ptak, Betty Grinzel, and Fran Ratajczak—for shouldering most of the burden in my absence back home in Grand Rapids during our recent trials and tribulations. Finally, but not lastly, I say thank you to my mother, Sophie Grinczel, from the bottom of my heart and the depths of my soul for your unfailing support, undeserved patience, and unrequited indulgence. Rest in peace, Gentle One.

—S. G.

**I**'d like to thank Mike Pearson of Sports Publishing for persuading me to believe that my story would be one folks would be interested in reading. I'd like thank all of my teammates through the years, all of my coaches, and all of my teachers, professors, family, and friends for their support, guidance, direction, and love. I certainly also want to thank Steve Grinczel for his diligence in working on this project.

—G. K.

# 1

# CULTURE SHOCK

## LIVING IN THE
## COMFORT ZONE

S ix years after becoming the head basketball coach at Michigan State University in 1969, Gus Ganakas had designs on taking a program with unremarkable tradition and which had enjoyed only sporadic success in its first 75 seasons to new heights. Coach Ganakas lured me to MSU with the promise I would be the cornerstone of a national championship team.

Of course, that expectation depended largely on the fruitful recruitment of a certain other player with a magical game—and matching nickname—who was playing his high school ball in Michigan State's backyard. But Coach Ganakas was charming, dressed well, and had leading-man good looks. His chief assistant and my primary recruiter was Vernon Payne, whom I liked a lot and my father liked even more. Why not Michigan State? It was an easy sell to an impressionable 17-year-old in 1975.

Coach Ganakas was impossible not to like. He was charismatic, witty, and some might even say gentle, but he was by no means soft. I remember him telling me, "If you come to Michigan State, I'll guarantee you one thing: you'll start on the roster behind the student manager and work your way up from there. But we believe you have the potential to do that." Being the son of a military man, I even liked that about him. Nevertheless, I was stunned the first time Coach Ganakas and Vernon screamed at me, because I was so used to them being smiley and friendly. Some people think Coach Ganakas was a pushover, but he'd get in our face and drive us. He might not have been as bombastic as some other coaches, but he'd get his point across.

The other assistant coaches were shooting guru Pat Miller, who likes to take credit for being the first to discover me, and Dick Versace, who later coached for years in the NBA. I liked all of them. The stars for Michigan State were Terry Furlow, Bob Chapman, Benny White, and Edgar Wilson, and most of them were juniors and seniors.

With his leading-man looks and sartorial splendor, Gus Ganakas oozed charisma as a recruiter and while coaching from the Michigan State bench. Amiable off the court, Coach Gus was all business on it and saw a national championship in MSU's future.
*Photo courtesy of Michigan State University*

I cracked the starting lineup four games into my freshman season and ended up averaging close to 12 points and 10 rebounds a game. With every passing day I told myself, "I can do this. I can play with these guys. I belong here."

I was in a good place, or so it seemed.

# THE WALKOUT AND THE WINDS OF CHANGE

When my freshman year ended, it felt good to say, "I am a Big Ten player. I am a Big Ten student." I could foresee only bigger and better things coming my way. What I didn't realize was that the beginning of the end had started for Coach Ganakas way back in January of '75, when I was still a senior in high school.

Ten African American players staged a walkout just hours before MSU's Big Ten home opener against No. 1–ranked Indiana. The players were ostensibly protesting Coach's decision to shake up the lineup. It was, however, really about much deeper issues than that. Coach Ganakas and his staff scrambled to fill the vacant spots with junior varsity guys. In the meantime, the rebellious players had a change of heart and came back hoping to undo the damage, but Coach Ganakas wouldn't let them play. Michigan State lost to the Hoosiers by a score of 107–55 in what became a national embarrassment for him and the university during racially tense times in America.

Coach Ganakas dealt sternly with the revolt, which reportedly erupted primarily over the players' perception they were second-class citizens as compared to MSU football players. He defused the situation as quickly as possible and meted out discipline, and the players apologized. I remember reading about and watching the news on it. Coach Gus was a great guy and a fine coach who had given many of those players opportunities they might not have otherwise gotten. So it was always perplexing to me that they chose to put him at risk.

I'm really glad I wasn't a part of it. Years later, I was talking to Benny White and some of the other players and found out that not all 10 guys involved in the walkout were in agreement. Some, such as Edgar Wilson, had serious apprehensions about whether it was the appropriate action to take, but in the end, perhaps feeling pressure from the team leaders, all 10 walked. I told Benny that I felt strongly that had I been a member of that team and truly disagreed, I would not have done it. I want to believe that I would have been my own man.

I can't truly say what I would have really done, however, because I wasn't in any of their shoes. Benny, Edgar Wilson, and the rest all tell me, "You just don't know what it was like. You would have had to be there. You had to experience the climate in which we were playing. You would have done it. You would have walked." After I got older, I came to realize that those players made an unbelievably serious decision that had grave consequences for livelihoods and careers.

A lot of them say it wasn't anything personal toward Coach Gus, it was personal toward the system, the racial atmosphere on campus, and too many complex issues to be able to pin it to just one thing. What's often forgotten is that they came back strong from it. After the players served their suspension, the team got back together and finished the season quite well. The Spartans won 10 of their last 17 games to finish 17-9 overall and fifth in the Big Ten with a 10-8 record.

When I arrived on campus, however, the walkout continued to hang over the athletic department. It was strange, because with the exception of Terry Furlow, who was cited as a catalyst in the incident, most of the guys who had major roles—like Lindsay Hairston and Bill Glover—were gone. Coach Ganakas got a one-year contract extension, and MSU went 14-13, and 10-8 in the Big Ten for the second straight season. We ended up all alone in fourth place for Coach Ganakas' best conference showing in his six seasons as head coach. I thought our semisuccessful year put the controversy behind us for good, and I fully expected Coach Ganakas to be back in 1976–1977.

My optimism was hopelessly misguided. Shortly after my freshman season came to a close, the MSU administration decided to make a clean sweep of the athletic department and fired Coach Ganakas. That was earth-shattering to me.

## I'M GETTING OUT OF HERE

Losing Coach Ganakas was a terrible jolt, because I wanted to play for him. The uncertainty was agonizing. I didn't know what was in store for Vernon Payne. There I was with three more years to go, and I had to play for someone I may not have wanted to play for had I been recruited by him. I starting to think, "Where can I transfer to?"

The University of Detroit, with Dick Vitale as the head coach, was still recruiting me. I actually thought about, "How could I get to Michigan?" because I wanted to stay near home, in the Big Ten, and I wanted to win. But if I had switched to another Big Ten school, I would have had to sit out a season under the NCAA transfer rule, forfeit a year of eligibility, and I couldn't be on scholarship. I was looking at UCLA where I would have played for Gene Bartow. My mind-set was, "I'm getting out of here."

After what I did as a freshman in a league that sent two teams, Indiana and Michigan, to the national championship game, I could have gotten in anywhere. Far more teams would have been interested in me coming out of MSU than when I was in high school. I had options. What team wouldn't want a guy who could do what I had just done as a freshman in the Big Ten?

# THE HEATHCOTE ERA BEGINS, DON'T TAKE IT PERSONAL

Before I was able to stage my own walkout, something remarkable happened. Coach Ganakas called me into his office and sat me down. We talked about the season and my role at Michigan State. But what struck me at the time, and has stayed with me ever since, was Coach Ganakas saying, "Greg, regardless of whether I'm here or not, this is where you belong."

Those words hit me like a sledgehammer. Coach Ganakas just got dumped by MSU without ceremony. He was at the absolute abyss of his career, and yet he spoke on behalf of the university and how important it was that I stay. That helped me sort through things, and told me even more about him. I already had a great deal of affection for Gus, but that took it into the stratosphere. A lot of fired coaches would have encouraged my desire to leave and said, "Sure, go someplace else. What do I care?"

When MSU eventually named Jud Heathcote to be the new head coach, I had no clue who he was, but that didn't last. I soon started hearing things such as "He's never coached any black players," "He's from the Pacific Northwest and doesn't know anything about the Midwest," "He's coming from that basketball mecca, the University of Montana," and "Man, are you guys ever in for a big change."

When I first met with Coach Heathcote in his office, his legendary sense of humor was in overdrive, and he was joking like he does. Boy, was that a smoke screen. The minute practice started, he started, and it was really, really hard to like Coach. I most certainly didn't like the style he brought with him from Montana. Everything was negative—every second of every minute of every day.

I know he had been forewarned that he was coming to Michigan State, "where they've got these black players who are out of control." I'm sure he was told that "You're going to have to go in there like a prison warden, lay down the law, be firm, and keep your foot down on those guys." And that's how he came in.

It was culture shock, because Coach Ganakas hadn't been like that. Coach Heathcote was one of those guys who, especially early on, demanded things operate his way and no other way. Every man had to get on his wavelength, or he was out of there.

I remember talking to my dad, Walter Kelser, about the situation. I am, however, the son of a military man who understood discipline, and I didn't get a whole lot of sympathy. He just encouraged me to hang in there, to work hard, and to try to do what the man was saying. That's what I did, but there were some instances when I thought Coach crossed the line.

I remember him warning us as a group, a day or two before his first practice, about how he coaches. At one point he singled out Tanya Webb, a sophomore center. "Tanya, if I say to you, 'Dammit, Tanya, you're the worst center I've ever seen,' I'm not really calling you the worst center," Coach Heathcote said. "You just can't take it personal."

Bob Chapman, who could find humor in almost any situation, quipped, "Why shouldn't he take it personal? It's not like Coach is lying."

And I was thinking to myself, "What the hell . . . ? I've got to deal with this for the next three years?"

# 2

# COCONUTS, BASKETBALLS, AND SPARTANS

## LEARNING TO ADAPT

**W**alter Kelser was my dad first and foremost, but he was also a staff sergeant in the U.S. Air Force. In late 1965, he received a two-and-a-half-year assignment to Okinawa. I was eight years old and very portable. Prior to that, we were stationed in San Antonio, Texas, and before that, we lived in Panama City, Florida. Lyndon Johnson was president, Martin Luther King Jr. was nearing the pinnacle of his prominence, and the civil rights movement was in full swing.

Even at my young age, I had a pretty good idea that when we left the United States for somewhere in the South Pacific, communications were going to be all but cut off. It wasn't like today when you can pick up a cell phone while driving down the street and call someone at the North Pole, or send an e-mail to someone on the other side of the world in a couple of seconds. At the time, there weren't many telephone conversations held between folks in Okinawa and Florida. You kept in touch by writing letters that you put in a mailbox. I wasn't happy about going to this distant island, even if it was a tropical paradise. I didn't like it at all.

But when you're eight, you gotta go when your mom and dad say go. Up until that time, I was an only child, but my mom, Verna, was pregnant with my younger brother, Raymond, and he was due for a December debut. By the time she gave birth in Panama City, my dad was already in Okinawa. After spending seven months in Florida, we joined my dad in July of '66. Of course, it took forever to get there. We flew to San Francisco, then Hawaii, and then to Okinawa.

It was a beautiful place, sunny and tropical, but being so far away from home and family was tough. Fortunately, like most people who are in the military and move from place to place a lot, we always met people and made new friends, which tended to soften the blow of being uprooted. We adapted to our environment and learned to make the most of it. I went to American schools, and when I was living on the base, it was like being in America for the most part, except for television.

We only got one station: channel 8 from AFRTS, which stands for Armed Forces Radio Television Services. We'd get shows from the States like *Gunsmoke* and *Bonanza.* A real popular show at the time was *The Fugitive.* On weekends we'd get sporting events, although they were never live. We'd get a college basketball or football game on Saturday, and a pro game on Sunday. That's how we were able to keep up with what was going on.

That's also when I first became aware of Bill Russell and the Boston Celtics, and Wilt Chamberlain and the Philadelphia 76ers. It seemed like they played against each other every Sunday. I'll never forget watching the games on the black and white TV, and on the bottom of the screen they'd have BOS and PHILA, and the score underneath. I was enthralled with Bill Russell.

# MAKING A LONG-DISTANCE CONNECTION

In November of '66, my dad was making a big deal out of an upcoming football game involving Michigan State and Notre Dame. My dad pulled for the Spartans because you sort of warmed to the organizations that provided opportunities for African Americans, and State was one of the earliest universities to do that. He said he was always a fan of Michigan State, but he never talked much about Michigan. I didn't understand the significance of the game in terms of one team being ranked No. 1 and the other No. 2, and that both teams were undefeated. I had no idea it was billed as "The Game of the Century" back in the States, but my dad really wanted Michigan State to win, and therefore, so did I.

We listened to the game on the radio at some crazy time of the day because of the time difference. For all I know, it might have been a taped replay, but I thought it was live, and we certainly listened to it as though it was. The game ended in a 10–10 tie, and as a nine-year-old I remember thinking, "Well, a tie isn't bad." But my dad was very disappointed with the way it turned out, and that always stayed with me. That's how Michigan State first became ingrained in my mind.

Of course, I had no way of knowing that a little more than 12 years later I would be playing in a game that had as much of an impact on the popularity of college basketball as the enduring MSU–Notre Dame tie had on the proliferation of college football.

# BASKETBALL IN PARADISE

Initially, I was all about football and we played a lot of it on the sandlot. I first developed my interest in basketball because my dad played on one of the Air Force base squads that competed in a seven-team league. I got a chance to see him play, go to his practices, and hang out with him and the guys on his team. They might as well have been in the NBA as far as I was concerned, because that's all I was exposed to, and those were the guys I looked up to.

When I was in the fourth grade, in the schoolyard we played what we passed off for basketball. We'd run up and down the court, shoot, and rebound. We didn't have to dribble, because none of us were able to. As time passed, we'd bounce the ball once or twice; and then four or five times; and the next thing we knew, we were comfortable with dribbling. There weren't any basketball camps like there are today. Basketball was self-taught.

We found out about the youth activities league at the neighboring Sukiran Army Base and I told my dad I wanted to play. My dad had never really seen me play and didn't know how good I was. Shoot, I didn't know how good I was, but I signed up for the 1967-68 season.

## AN EXOTIC INTRODUCTION TO THAT CHAMPIONSHIP FEELING

From the moment I started playing organized basketball, I had an idea that I was actually pretty good. I played for the Sukiran Bobcats, which was my first exposure to coaches, practices, and real games. Not to boast, but I was a star in the Elementary Division of the Fort Buckner Youth Basketball League. Our team went undefeated, and I led the league in scoring. I had a career-high 26 points in one game, and I was the league's most valuable player. I was maybe five feet tall, but completely unstoppable.

I was surprised by how easy basketball came to me. Like any other kid who watches sports on TV, I thought I was going to be able to play at the highest levels some day. You don't think of the overwhelming odds and stuff like that when you're 10.

## THE COLD SLAP OF REALITY

From Okinawa, we moved to Boston, where I spent my most difficult time as a youngster. We arrived there in September of 1968, just as my dad was beginning a tour of duty in a remote area of England. My mother had three sisters and two brothers living in Boston, and I still have family there. I was 11 years old and going into the sixth grade. It was very difficult being a young black kid in Boston in the '60s, but it continues to help shape who I am today.

I attended St. Peter's Catholic school in Dorchester. Out of the 600 some kids, there were three black students: two girls and me. Needless to say, a lot of the other kids weren't used to being around black people. I found myself fighting a lot because every time I was racially slurred—and it seemed to be every other day—my response was to fight. I often came home with holes in my pants and bruises on my face.

We lived in an area where hockey and baseball were big, but I still played organized basketball. My mom was working and my dad was overseas, so the only support I had at my games came from my coaches and teammates and the people who oversaw our school.

When we played at other schools, it was horrific. Wherever I went I was often called "nigger," "Sambo," "little jazzbo," and the adults did nothing to stop it. In fact, during my half-mile walk to school in the morning, it wasn't unusual for adults to roll down their car windows and say, "Hey little nigger boy, where you goin'?"

While living in Panama City, I had seen segregated facilities with my own eyes. I vividly recall "colored" and "white" drinking fountains side-by-side at the filling stations. My parents told me that when you see two fountains and one says "colored" and one says "white" don't drink out of either one of them. However, the racism I experienced in Boston was far worse than anything I had ever encountered in the Deep South.

Everybody loves Boston's history and New England atmosphere, but for me it represents something totally different. The natives in Okinawa treated me better than the Americans in Boston. Even to this day, Boston is one of my least favorite cities.

While I would never want anybody to go through it, the two years spent in Boston strengthened me, because I came out of there without hate for anyone, and the ability to not let the actions of a few represent a whole group in my mind. It was a part of my life that I have chosen not to forget. A few years ago I visited Dorchester, and while I retraced my old route to St. Peter's school, I quietly reflected on how thankful I am to come out of there without being a severely scarred individual, and how that experience affects the way I deal with people as an adult.

I look at our entire time in the Air Force as being wonderful in terms of exposing me to a lot of places and cultures. It was a great opportunity to meet people of various races and cultures, and to see how they live. It also taught me how to get along with everyone and look at others, regardless of their background, as just people, because that's how I want to be treated.

You might say I stood out while attending St. Peter's Elementary School in Dorchester, Massachusetts, but not because I was the tallest kid in my class. The difficult but invaluable lessons I learned about bigotry while living in the Boston area taught me to treat everyone I meet the way I would like to be treated, and continue to shape who I am today. I still enjoy talking to Sister Barbara (far right) from time to time.
*Photo courtesy of St. Peter School*

# THE LIFE OF AN AIR FORCE BRAT COMES TO AN END

My dad graduated from Detroit Northern High School in '54 and planned to settle our family down near his hometown after he retired from the Air Force. First we moved from the East Coast to Marysville, California; and then, in the summer of 1971, to Ferndale, Michigan. Dad was a tech sergeant by then and had roughly two years to go in the service with a tour of duty as a member of the military police coming up in Vietnam.

We purchased a house, but weren't going to close on it until January of '72, so I enrolled at this little school in Oak Park called Frost

Junior High. I was in the ninth grade and went there for three months. When our house was ready, I finished out the school year at Taft Middle School in Detroit. It was consistent with what I'd always done—going to two schools in one year.

When I finally got to Detroit Henry Ford High School in September of 1972, it was my 10th school in nine years; ranging from Florida, to Texas, to Okinawa, to Massachusetts, to California, and finally, Michigan. Switching schools in the middle of the year was nothing new to me. I went to three different schools in the second grade, three different schools in the eighth grade, and two different schools in the ninth grade, all because of the military.

What was unusual about Michigan was that I finally got the opportunity to stay at one school for three years. The timing was perfect, because if you're going to be an athlete, you need some stability, and I very much had the potential to be good basketball player in high school, and hopefully, beyond.

# A ROADBLOCK IN DETROIT

In my sophomore year at Henry Ford, I wasn't given the opportunity to try out for the varsity basketball team, because the coach at the time, Wes Carlos, was also the football coach. He already had his varsity basketball team set; out of the 14 guys on the team, seven were also on the football team. While they weren't necessarily better than me, they were mostly juniors and seniors. Coach Carlos wanted his football players to play sports all year round if they could, and if they had any basketball talent whatsoever, then they were on the team. There wasn't a spot for me, so I ended up playing on the junior varsity for that first semester.

In 1972, and even today, the high school games in the City of Detroit are played at 3:30 in the afternoon and the jayvees play afterward. The day of my very first game, the varsity played, and the gym was packed. As soon as the varsity game was over the place emptied out, and we played our jayvee game in front of maybe 30 or 40 people. That was my awakening to what jayvee truly was. It meant nothing to the fans, and that was disappointing. My whole way of thinking became: if I work hard and play well, they'll move me up to varsity.

# I CAN PLAY

I played pretty well on jayvee and started most of the games. When our season ended Coach Carlos promoted me to the varsity. I was real skinny, but I could jump and rebound. After riding the bench for two or three games, but playing well in practice and establishing the things I could get done, I was placed in the starting lineup just in time for the state tournament. It was a major development, because until then, I only got mop-up duty. I think they just finally decided, "Hey, we can use the kid's energy and rebounding."

At 6-foot-3 and about 170 pounds, I became our starting center. To that point, Henry Ford had never won so much as a district championship in the state tournament, but we began postseason play at North Farmington High School with a pretty good team. We won three games with me averaging nine points and around 13 rebounds, and we took the district.

Our first game in the regionals was against Detroit Catholic Central with Tom LaGarde, a 6-foot-10, 220-pound senior center headed to the University of North Carolina. He would later earn a spot on the 1976 U.S. Olympic team that would win the gold medal in Montreal. I was assigned to guard LaGarde, even though he was seven inches taller and 50 pounds heavier. Needless to say, we didn't fare too well, and Detroit Catholic Central beat us pretty easily. At the end of the game, I had six points, ten rebounds, and was in foul trouble. That's how our season ended, but it told me—and everybody around me— that "I can play, and if varsity's the highest level for me right now, I can play at that level."

# WINNING IS THE THING

We had six or seven seniors on the team the following season, and even though I was a junior it was clear that I was going to be one of the featured players. Not long after the 1973–1974 season had started, I realized that while I could get a lot of things done on the floor, we just weren't amassing victories the way I thought we should have. We were pretty much a .500 team the whole year, and I became very disappointed that we couldn't win more. Even as a 16-year-old junior, I knew the greatest recognition came not with just scoring a bunch of points, but with winning a lot of games.

That season ended disappointingly with us losing our very first game in the district tournament against Detroit Central. It was a bad situation all the way around. Earlier that day, I had skipped a class I thought I could afford to miss. Nonetheless, Coach Carlos punished me with a first-quarter benching, and we fell behind early. I went in at the beginning of the second quarter, played the rest of the game, and scored 28 points, but couldn't bring us back.

At that time, I began to think I should leave Henry Ford and go someplace else with a rich tradition—like Mumford—my senior year, because I wanted to win. During my junior season, our team had seven seniors, including three starters. I recall that one day at practice our coach had the underclassmen play the seniors in a scrimmage and we annihilated them. So I concluded, "You know what, we might not be too bad next year," and I stayed put.

# UNDERSTANDING MY WORTH

We had a pretty good team my senior year, and I averaged 24 points and 17 rebounds a game. Long before triple-doubles became a part of the Michigan State lexicon, I had 41 points, 29 rebounds, and 12 assists against Detroit Osborn. But in the district finals against Detroit Southeastern, I fouled out after scoring only 10 points, and our dream of winning a state championship was over. I felt responsible because we weren't a deep team and couldn't afford any of that.

I'll never forget that Tommie Wood, who would eventually referee some of my games in the NBA, officiated that game. We're friends to this day, but I never let him forget that at least two of those fouls were very questionable. He was on his climb up the ladder, too, reffing high school ball.

The only team success as a high school player that I can boast about is the district title we won my sophomore year after I got moved up from jayvee. I was all-city as a junior, and all-city and all-state as a senior, but something new came about that year.

*The Detroit News* selected the Class A Dream Team, which supposedly represented the best of the best in the state of

Michigan. It was comprised of: Bruce Flowers from Berkley High School who eventually went to Notre Dame; Terry Duerod, who went to the University of Detroit after winning a state championship with Highland Park High School; Alan Hardy of Detroit Northwestern who went to Michigan; and Ferndale's Tom Staton who went to Michigan.

The fifth member of that Dream Team, and who I felt was chosen probably to fill out his resume more than for any other reason because he was already all-state in football and baseball, was Rick Leach of Flint Southwestern High School. He also went to Michigan, were he became an All-America quarterback on the football team.

The only consolation for me once my high school career ended was that I was now heading to the next level at a major university in a major conference. As I look back on my high school career, if I had known a little bit more about Detroit high schools—keep in mind I had been in the state of Michigan less than a year when I enrolled at Henry Ford—I would have gone somewhere with a little more basketball history and tradition so I could have experienced winning at the ultimate level. I would have loved to have had city and state championships in addition to those I won at Michigan State.

And yet, Henry Ford only came into existence in 1957, and for its first 15 years it hadn't done anything in basketball until we finally got a district championship and had some fine seasons record-wise. One of the things I take solace in is that it happened when I was there.

## KELSER AND JOHNSON LINKED FOR THE FIRST TIME

I was third-team All-State as a senior and truly deserved better, but ironically enough there was a sophomore out of Lansing on that third-team as well—a fella by the name of Earvin "Magic" Johnson.

## DEVELOPING AN AFFINITY WITH MSU

My interest with Michigan State started with the football team in the '60s. When I moved to Michigan as a ninth-grader in late 1971, I had to wonder, "Where did State go?" I realized in short order that everything in the universe revolved around the University of Michigan—I mean everything! Consequently, that's what I geared myself towards. I cheered for the Wolverines because they had the better football program at that time and probably a better basketball program, too.

But I remember watching a Big Ten Basketball Game of the Week featuring Michigan State and Minnesota. Unlike now, when it seems every college game is televised, there wasn't a lot of basketball on TV. You might get one or two college games on Saturday, maybe one on Sunday, and certainly nothing during the week. I remember watching one particular game in which, from the top of the key, Spartan guard Bill Glover hit a shot right at the buzzer to win the game. I immediately became a fan of Michigan State basketball. It took something as simple as that.

Then, even before Michigan State was recruiting me, I remember watching the football game when the Spartans upset No. 1–ranked Ohio State in 1974. Levi Jackson took the ball 88 yards up the sideline, and then the Buckeyes scored a controversial touchdown as time expired. It seemed as though they'd won it, but Big Ten commissioner Wayne Duke and the game officials huddled for about an hour afterward and decided the touchdown didn't count, letting MSU pull off a mind-boggling upset.

I wasn't in Michigan State's sights when those things were going on, but we seemed to be made for each other.

# 3

# GETTING DISCOVERED

## IS ANYBODY OUT THERE WATCHING?

I got my first recruiting letter between my junior and senior year at Henry Ford High School in Detroit. It wasn't like it is now with players being recruited by eighth and ninth grade. I wasn't as acutely aware of recruiters eyeing my every move as top players are nowadays. When those kids play a game now, they know there are probably five or six college recruiters up in the stands watching them. I think a large part of recruiting back when I played was accomplished through word of mouth, gathering information on the top 20 players in a certain area or city, and then maybe visiting them in person. There certainly wasn't much film on us. I don't remember seeing a single high school game I played on tape. Not one.

## FINALLY, SOME NAME RECOGNITION

Heidelberg College, a little school in Ohio, was the first to write to me. It was in the summer of 1974, and I remember being real excited about that, because at least I was being recruited. At least somebody was noticing my ability and feeling I might be able to help their team, and that I might get a scholarship.

Shortly after that, the University of Minnesota started recruiting me right at the beginning of my senior year, long before the basketball season was to start. That made me realize I might have some real talent, because Minnesota was in the Big Ten and everybody knew about the Golden Gophers. Plus they had a good team throughout the early '70s. I didn't know how Minnesota's coaches knew about me, because I was never aware of their presence at my games. In fact, I don't think they'd ever been to one. I was always curious to find out, "How does Minnesota even know I can play, or how I might be able to fit in?"

But they recruited me rigorously, and I took my first official visit to Minnesota. An assistant coach by the name of Jimmy Williams, who was a great guy, recruited me. Bill Musselman was the head coach. Current Detroit Pistons coach Flip Saunders was a star guard, and I was hosted by Gopher all-time great Mychal Thompson. I remember meeting football quarterback Tony Dungy, who is now the coach of the Indianapolis Colts. I really had a great time during my visit to Minneapolis in October of 1974, and I remember thinking to myself, "Well you know what, at the very least if no one else comes after me, I can go here," because they made if very clear to me they wanted me.

## SOMETHING'S ROTTEN IN MINNESOTA

A couple weeks after I got back from visiting the University of Minnesota, my parents and I got a visit from an NCAA investigator. This was strange, because he showed up on our doorstep in the middle of the night. I had an after-school job at a Hardee's restaurant on the corner of 8 Mile Road and Redfern Street in Detroit. I worked the evening shift from 5 p.m. to 11 p.m. I was making two dollars an hour and would eventually get a raise of five cents. Hey, consider the times.

I got home from work at around 11:30 p.m. Not much later, there was a knock on the front door. How often does that happen at 12:30 a.m.? My dad opened the door and there was a guy who identified himself as an investigator from the NCAA office in Kansas

City and wanted to talk about my visit to Minnesota. He wanted to know everything that happened, whether I was offered any money, given any additional gifts, were any promises made to me? The answers were: "No, no and no."

He spent a considerable amount of time with us nonetheless, and through our conversation we found out his visit was just a part of a larger investigation probing the University of Minnesota basketball program. He even intimated to us that there had been improprieties going on for some time and that there were going to be sanctions. He just didn't know how many or when.

I immediately became dismayed about that, because I didn't want to play someplace that might be going on probation. As it turned out, their basketball program ended up getting a three-year probation similar to what Michigan State had received for their football program in 1976. That season, the Gophers finished 24-3 but had to forfeit all of their wins and were banned from postseason play because of NCAA sanctions.

## SPARTAN INTRODUCTION

Michigan State came into the fold in December of 1974. Henry Ford was playing in a Christmas tournament against Northwestern High School, which was *the* premier high school in terms of basketball talent in the City of Detroit. They had this guy named Alan Hardy, who Michigan State—along with everyone else—was recruiting. Minnesota had Alan in the week before my visit. So MSU assistant coach Vernon Payne came down to see Alan, and he had 29 points and eight rebounds. He played well and they beat us by three. I had 28 points and 18 rebounds, but the thing that most impressed Vernon Payne was my willingness to dive on the floor for loose balls. That's how Michigan State became aware of the fact I even existed.

Michigan only casually recruited me. I never took a visit there and they only sent me a letter, which I put in a big box with all the other letters—most of which I never opened. A few years later, while I was at State, I just happened to open that envelope from Michigan and in it were a note from Wolverine head coach Johnny Orr and a pair of tickets to a game. I guess I missed it.

# RECRUITING GAME ON

Vernon Payne was a very dynamic guy, and he came to many of my games after that first one and met my parents. He and my father immediately clicked. In fact, there were times Vernon would come down to Detroit just to hang out with my dad. Sometimes I would come home from school and see Vernon's car in the driveway, and I would be confused because I didn't have a game that day. Well, my dad had a bar in the basement, and Vernon would be down there just schmoozing with my dad. The rules were a lot different then. He and my dad became pretty close, and it was obvious Michigan State was recruiting my father, although Vernon made it very clear to me that Michigan State would be offering me a scholarship.

# GUS GANAKAS, A MAN OF FAITH

It's amazing how recruiting has changed over the years. Can you imagine Tom Izzo taking a kid he's never seen play? I didn't meet Michigan State head coach Gus Ganakas until later, and I liked him, too, but Coach Gus never came to a single one of my games. He would come down with Vernon to hang out with my dad, but he never saw me play. He went on Vernon's word. I remember being so overwhelmed by Vernon, and then eventually Coach Ganakas who was just this charming person.

There were all these other factors in Michigan State's favor—my dad loving Michigan State, the engaging personalities Vernon and Gus presented, Minnesota being in trouble, and Michigan showing very little interest.

# NOT QUITE A DONE DEAL

Although I was really leaning toward Michigan State, I took two more visits. I went to Arizona State, and tried to go out there with an open mind. Arizona State was fascinating, because the day I left Michigan it was about 10 degrees, and when I arrived in Tempe it was 79. And ASU was in the NCAA Tournament.

The Sun Devils were playing a first-round game that weekend, and they had me in town along with James Hardy, who ended up going to the University of San Francisco and played with the Utah Jazz; Paul Mokeski who went to Kansas before playing a number of years in the NBA; and a guy named Flinty Ray Williams, who ended up going to UNLV. We watched Arizona State play in its home arena against Alabama and All-America center Leon Douglas.

Experiencing that whole atmosphere—it was sunny and beautiful, a wonderful arena, good teams in the NCAA Tournament—was pretty impressive. Plus, I had an aunt and uncle stationed at a nearby Air Force base. If I wouldn't have gone to Michigan State, I'm pretty sure Arizona State would have been my choice. In fact, it was so nice that I stayed an extra day.

My next visit to Central Michigan was really as a courtesy to Ben Kelso, who was an assistant coach at Henry Ford during my senior year before becoming a hugely successful head coach at Detroit Cooley. Central recruited me pretty heavily, and since Ben was a former Chippewa, I had to go visit. I also took a little visit to the University of Detroit, because it was a local school and I went to a lot of their games. In the end though, I wanted to play in the Big Ten or another major conference.

# A TALE OF BETRAYAL

Alan Hardy, my rival at Detroit Northwestern, and I became pretty good friends during our senior year of high school. We talked frequently, and since a lot of the same schools were recruiting both of us, we had decided to compare notes. We surmised that it might be a good idea to go to the same school because we would have a chance to play together, and an even better chance to win. We talked about Michigan State, Minnesota, U of D, Central Michigan, and various other schools that were interested in both of us. Alan liked Vernon Payne and MSU, and so did I.

In late March of 1975, after our senior seasons had ended, Alan and I were playing for the Detroit AAU team at a tournament in Sharon, Pennsylvania. There were teams from throughout the nation. Bill Cartwright was there along with Albert King, the younger brother of Bernard King, and all the top players from Detroit. Vernon was there as well. Alan and I were roommates, and on Saturday night after the tournament had ended we were in our hotel room preparing to for the trip home when Vernon paid a visit.

He spoke to us for a long time about how much he wanted us and how good Michigan State would be if both of us went there. After Vernon left, Alan and I talked at length about what he said. We concluded that we both liked Michigan State, so we might as well go ahead with our plan.

We called Vernon at his hotel and said, "Coach, we're going to sign with MSU." He was ecstatic. He had run back to our hotel room, congratulated us and told us that we had made a great decision. As Vernon left, he had told us that he'd see us Monday morning to sign our letters for the Big Ten. Back then you had to sign a conference letter and a national letter for the school you chose. The Big Ten letter was binding in the sense that you couldn't sign with another Big Ten school; however, the loophole was that you were still able to sign with a school in another conference.

Vernon showed up at my house first because he passed it first on his way in from East Lansing. I signed my letter and he left to get Alan's signature. About an hour later I got a phone call from Vernon. The instant I heard the tone of his voice I knew Alan didn't sign with MSU. Vernon said Alan decided he wanted to wait because apparently Bobby Knight had called from Indiana and he was going to consider that possibility.

I was very disappointed because we had agreed to go as a package. Even as a 17-year-old, I understood how important it was to hold up one's end of the bargain, and after talking to Alan about it for the past four months, I thought we had a deal. I felt that at the very least, he could have called me before I had signed to let me know that he had changed his mind. But he hadn't, and Vernon went back to East Lansing with one signature.

## SIGNING DAY NO. 2

I had already signed the Big Ten letter locking me into Michigan State, but I still could have gone to Arizona State or any other school from a different league. The situation was pretty interesting on national signing day a couple of weeks later.

While I worked the night shift at the Hardee's, Vernon Payne was waiting at my house with his signed conference letter-of-intent, along with an assistant coach from Arizona State, an assistant coach from Central Michigan, and one of the assistants from the University of Detroit.

I wasn't looking forward to going home, because somebody was going to leave disappointed. Vernon got tired of waiting. He had excused himself, not telling the others where he was going and came to the Hardee's restaurant. When I saw him come in, I went up to the counter and said, "Can I help you?"

I was being a smart aleck.

He said, "I'll have a Coke and a signature."

I got him his Coke and he said, "Greg, where do you want to go? You know you want to be a Spartan."

I was ready and wanted to get it over with. I signed it right there on the Hardee's counter. He took the letter back my house and later my dad told me he was grinning from ear to ear. I stayed at Hardee's, because I still had three or four hours to go on my shift.

It was quite a bit different than the way kids do it today. Now there are press conferences in their high school gyms in front of the student body and maybe even before a television audience.

Later, Denny Alexander from Central Michigan came to the restaurant to offer his congratulations, but said he was very disappointed although he understood my decision. He was very gracious. It was difficult to be 17 and in a situation like that because I knew I was letting down people who had spent a great deal of time courting me and whom I had grown to like.

## SIGNED, SEALED, AND DELIVERED—SITE UNSEEN

No one's ever heard me rave about my MSU recruiting visit, because I didn't take one. Coach Gus and Vernon had convinced me to become a Spartan even though I had never laid eyes on the MSU campus. I had heard about Jenison Field House, the home of the

Spartans, but never saw it in person. What I knew about my prospective teammates was based on what I read in the paper or saw on TV. I had signed completely based on my confidence in Coach Ganakas and Vernon. They had calmed whatever apprehension I had about anything. I wanted to play for them in the worst way. Had they been at the University of Michigan and were recruiting me out of Detroit Henry Ford High School the way they did, I would have been at Michigan. My ongoing, long-time connection to MSU is truly the benefit of a relationship with those two men.

## GETTING ACQUAINTED

I did eventually visit the campus, but it was after I signed. I brought my parents there to show them around. We stayed in the Kellogg Center, MSU's on-campus hotel, toured the library and some of the other places. Jenison Field House was the last place we went.

I wouldn't say I was relieved when I saw how beautiful the campus was in springtime; overwhelmed was more like it. It was huge, and 40,000-plus students went there.

That evening I went to some parties with Terry Furlow, Benny White, and Bob Chapman. They couldn't have been better hosts. They embraced me from that moment on. Nothing remarkable happened at the parties, but I did realize that Terry was a big man on campus. Everyone knew him, and it enhanced the aura I already thought he had.

I left MSU thinking, "This is a big place, and it's going to be my challenge to not get lost and swallowed up." The size of the campus and the large student population intimidated me. When I went to Henry Ford, I was a nobody and had to work my way onto the varsity. I was worried the same thing was going to happen at Michigan State. I had confidence in my ability, but I had no idea how things would work out.

I played with a lot of college guys the summer before my freshman year at MSU and held my own. It helped me gain confidence that I could do it once I got on campus.

# ALMOST NOT A SPARTAN

Michigan State was on the quarter system, so school didn't start until late September. Although I had signed a letter-of-intent, I still had to apply for admission. I submitted my application, and I thought it was just a formality. However, I got a letter from the university admissions office in June rejecting my application. Whoever wrote it apologized and said that I wasn't accepted. It may have had something to do with my ACT score. I took the test the morning after my high school's prom so I hadn't been very into it. Back then they didn't put weight on the test, because you didn't need it to get into college. I didn't care about it, and probably didn't do too well. I never even saw the results of the test. I had figured that I would be okay because I had a 3.0 GPA and that was just from going to class. I never had to study much because high school had come easily.

Well, I panicked and called Vernon Payne. He told me to relax and stop worrying. A week later I got a letter that read, "Congratulations, you have been accepted."

I should have kept that first letter and had it framed. I could have hung it next to my Academic All-America plaque.

# WELCOME TO MSU

When I arrived on campus to stay, my parents dropped me off at Emmons Hall in the Brody Complex. We unloaded all my stuff from the trunk of the car and they left. I was on my own. I was sad and really nervous because I didn't know what the hell to expect. When I went to my first class I found that that I was already behind. I was supposed to have already completed some reading, but I had never received a syllabus. I thought, "How am I going to survive four years up here?" It just seemed like there was so much more responsibility than before, and school was no joke.

I had all these things going on in my head, and I was a little homesick. Even though home was only 70 miles away, it might as well have been 700. The one thing that helped center me was playing ball after class at Jenison Field House before official practice began. When I was nestled inside those four black lines it didn't seem like I was at a big university or away from home. I was back in familiar surroundings—on the basketball court.

Regardless of where the court is, it gives me a sense of serenity, and that helps me tremendously. In college, I used it to my advantage. I wondered how other students who didn't have something like that to embrace made the transition to college life. I suppose that's why so many pledge fraternities or join clubs and organizations that interest them—it allows you to shrink such a monstrous place. Getting into basketball helped make MSU's size seem less daunting to me. Every day that I played with the guys made me feel more and more like I belonged and could be successful.

## THE MSU RECRUIT CLASS OF 1975

I came in with Tanya Webb, who was from Augusta, Arkansas. He was one of the top players in the state, 6-foot-8, 240 pounds, and chiseled from solid rock. He was a power forward/center. Another member of my class was Milton Wiley, a 6-foot, sharp-shooting guard from Belleville, Illinois. The other guy was Paul Stoll, a transfer from Lansing Community College. I roomed with Milton and Tanya at Emmons Hall, and we built a loft with two beds up and one down. Space was minimal at the beginning, but it got better as students dropped out. I had a single by the spring term.

I was at Jenison every day, and I could really fly. One time I hit my head on the backboard when I went up to block a shot, and everybody thought that was a big deal. The first thing that struck me, other than the backboard, was the coaches saying I was a good defender, because I had never really fashioned myself as a defensive player. My thing was scoring when I came out of Henry Ford, but what made me stand out at MSU was the fact that I could rebound against anybody.

# GOOD TIMING

My first year at MSU was only the third season that freshmen were eligible to play. I was really happy about that, because I felt like if I had the ability then I should be able to compete at the varsity level as opposed to wasting a year on a freshman squad.

# PLAYING TIME

My first game was on December 1, 1975, against Central Michigan. I came off the bench in the second half. I didn't score—it was the only one of my 115 games as a Spartan in which that happened—but I had five rebounds and a blocked shot in seven minutes.

It was Tanya Webb who came off the bench and really saved us. He moved people around and bulled his way to the basket. He had nine points in 11 or 12 minutes.

Tanya had a Southern drawl and was funny and crazy. The day after the game he was suddenly real popular. Everybody was giving him accolades for his big performance and women were falling all over him. So he dumped his girlfriend Debbie. He told her now that he was on the basketball team there were going to be a lot of women coming around, and he didn't want to see her get hurt. He had explained that the best thing for them to do was to break up because he was going to have to pay attention to these women. Debbie, of course, was crushed.

Our next game was at Eastern Michigan, and Tanya got in, but he didn't do anything. He went from nine to zero. The next day he got back with Debbie. Amazingly, she took him back.

# GOING AGAINST NORTHERN MICHIGAN AND TOM IZZO

I came off the bench against Eastern Michigan and scored 13 points, blocked three shots, and had seven rebounds. I got in the next games against Canisius and Western Michigan as well.

My first start came against Northern Michigan with a nifty little point guard named Tom Izzo, who became the Spartan head coach 20 years later. I remember we won the game, but of course didn't know who Tom was. I didn't have to guard him because I was a forward and he was a about a foot shorter. I started the rest of my career—111 straight games—and little Tommy Izzo became a Division II All-American.

# MAKING THE TRANSITION

My transition to being a starter was easy, because everybody embraced me and really liked me. Terry Furlow took me under his wing as did the other upperclassmen—Benny White, Edgar Wilson, Bob Chapman, and Lovelle Rivers.

I mention Lovelle because he was a senior forward and hoped to start. I roomed with Lovelle a lot on the road, and will forever be indebted to him because he used to talk to me and help me out. He'd always tell me about the people I was assigned to guard in the upcoming game. I never understood at that particular time why he would be so willing to help a skinny freshman who was taking playing time away from him. He was such an amazing individual because he thought enough of the team to help me succeed as much as he could. That was symbolic of the way they all treated me.

# LEARNING ON THE GO

All freshman athletes had study hall from eight to ten o'clock four nights a week. The only way you could get out of it was by attaining a 2.5 grade-point average or better, or you'd be back in there for the second term. Clarence Underwood, who later worked as a deputy commissioner in the Big Ten office before becoming MSU's athletic director, was the person you had to answer to if you didn't go. He was an intimidating, no-nonsense guy who didn't smile a whole lot.

Kirk Gibson and Eugene Byrd from the football team were in there as well. I figured that since I had to be there, I should make the best of it and bring some books. That helped me develop study habits I hadn't had in high school. I got my GPA up to 2.9, and I was out of there.

# BREAKING OUT
# AS A DIAPER DANDY

At 6-foot-6, 185 pounds, I wasn't very big, but Coach Ganakas played me at the center spot because I could defend and rebound. I didn't get a lot of shots, and there certainly weren't any plays run for me, but I was able to run the floor and get shots off the offensive window. Before long, I was averaging double figures in rebounding and scoring.

My breakout game as a scorer was against Dick Vitale's University of Detroit team in Cobo Arena, which, at the time, was the home of the Detroit Pistons. Vitale looked at the matchup as an opportunity to stick it to Michigan State and garner attention for his program. They did beat us by three points, but Terry Furlow had an amazing game. He scored 41 points.

I had 17 points, which was my career high at that point, and it came in my hometown, which really made me feel good. I was just disappointed we lost the game. My role was solidified, and I knew what I had to do to stay in the starting lineup and be a factor. Terry Furlow was our scorer, Bob Chapman was our No. 2 option, Benny White was our ball-handler and playmaker, and Edgar Wilson was another scorer. I rebounded, played defense, and scored when I got the opportunity.

# A STUNNING BIG TEN DEBUT

Kyle Macy scored 38 points in his first Big Ten game for Purdue, which is where he played before he transferred to Kentucky. When I heard about this, I thought, "My goodness, a freshman scoring 38 points. That's pretty doggone good." I'm not saying that it motivated me, because I knew I wasn't going to score 38 points in my first league game, but I was really anticipating the opener at the University of Wisconsin.

We played horribly as a team and didn't shoot the ball well. However, we shot so poorly—29 percent from the floor—that I was able to get 12 offensive rebounds and 27 total. Although that's my all-time high at MSU and is fifth all-time in school history, I didn't think it was that big of a deal when I did it. After all, I had a record of 29 rebounds in a high school game. I figured I'd be able to do it all the time in college, but I never even got close again. The most I had after that was 16.

I played all 40 minutes against the Badgers that night, and afterward Terry Furlow said, "Young Fella showed out, but I'll have something for you the next game." We headed home to play Iowa, and I wondered if Terry would be a man of his word.

At a skinny 6-foot-6½ and 185 pounds, I wasn't your prototypical Big Ten center, but that's where I began my career and made the first of 111 consecutive starts.
*Photo courtesy of Michigan State University*

# FURLOW'S FURIOUS TRIFECTA

Terry had a three-game stretch no other player has ever had, or probably ever will, at Michigan State. He put 50 on Iowa in a 105–88 win to set a school record, which he still holds. It would have been 55 or 56 if the three-point line had been in effect, because he was knocking them down from way out. Three days later, Terry got 48 in a 105–89 loss to Northwestern; and two days after that, he had 42 in a 92–82 victory over Ohio State. That's 140 points in six days, nearly 47 points per game.

Meanwhile, I was just doing my rebounding thing and led the Big Ten with nearly 13 caroms per game for most of the season. Minnesota's Mychal Thompson—a true center—overtook me late in the year. I finished second to him with 11 per game.

# SETTING GOALS

When Terry Furlow broke Mike Robinson's MSU career scoring record of 1,717 points later in the 1975-76 season, I remember thinking to myself, "I'm going to break his record," which ended up being 1,777 points. I also thought that I would break Johnny Green's rebounding record of 1,036 set in 1959 because I had gotten off to a great start. Gus Ganakas kept his word when he said I'd have to work my way up from the bottom, but he had a lot of confidence in me. He weathered the mistakes any freshman would make, and he gave me an opportunity to play.

There were plenty of nights when I'd play all 40 minutes, some when I'd play 36, some when I'd play 30, and others when I'd play 25, but I was in the starting lineup to stay. I've always considered the fact that my teammates accepted me, didn't resent me, and tried to help me as a major factor in my development as a player. Not all freshmen get that support from their older teammates

My parents were at every home game and the road games that were nearby. I had gone to Michigan State so that they could see me play. Had I gone to Arizona State, they would not have been able to come to my games regularly, and I really enjoyed having them there for me.

# A HOUSE DIVIDING

Before I signed for Michigan State, I had been given every indication that Coach Ganakas would be with the team all four years, and that made me feel comfortable enrolling as a freshman.

We had an average season that year, and didn't get invited to play in a postseason tournament. We were 14-13 overall, but 10-8 in the Big Ten. That isn't bad considering that's the year Indiana and Michigan met in the national championship game. Half of our conference losses were against the Hoosiers, who finished the season with a 32-0 record, and the Wolverines, who went 25-7 after losing in the NCAA final.

We finished fourth in the Big Ten. By today's standards, MSU would have been NCAA Tournament-worthy, but the field was limited to 32 teams back then. If we had won our last game against Wisconsin instead of losing 86–82, we probably would have gone to the NIT, which was still a big deal, because the NCAA was so limited.

The walkout still loomed large, but I thought when we cleared .500 Coach Ganakas would still be safe. Michigan State wasted no time, however. We got a new athletic director with a mandate to clean house, and that's what Joe Kearny did. Denny Stolz was out as the MSU football coach as well. I thought Coach Gus got a raw deal.

# ALAN HARDY POSTSCRIPT

Alan Hardy ended up going to Michigan and played sparingly as a freshman. I don't mean to sound vindictive, but both times we played the Wolverines, I enjoyed seeing him sit on their bench. We never really spoke to each other about him reneging on our agreement. In fact, our friendship ceased to exist after he didn't sign with MSU. Alan was a good jump-shooter, but he wasn't the most physical guy in the world, and he wasn't a good rebounder.

I wasn't a big guy, but no one could ever call me soft. I was physical, which is the way you needed to be to have the kind of instant success in the Big Ten that I enjoyed. I didn't mind taking punishment, but I certainly also tried to dish it out, especially against Alan Hardy whenever I saw him, because I had held onto the betrayal I felt. But I got beyond it a long time ago; I like Alan a lot.

# 4

# A PROGRAM TAKES SHAPE

## DUNK YOU VERY MUCH FOR MORE GOOD TIMING

**W**hen I arrived at State, the dunk had been outlawed in college basketball since the 1967-68 season. No matter how high you could fly and stay up in the air, at some point you had to turn the wrist over and let the ball fall through the hoop. David Thompson and Monte Towe patented that alley-oop lob at North Carolina State, but no matter how high David got up he still had to kiss the ball off the glass or drop it in—he couldn't thump it.

The NCAA reinstated the dunk during the spring term of my freshman year. When I got the news I started jumping up and down. It was big for me, because dunking gave me an opportunity to be a more effective scorer. I used to dunk in high school games and take the technical foul when games were out of reach. Now I could dunk for real.

# SPRINGTIME/SUMMERTIME JUD

When Coach Heathcote was hired, we got the "Springtime/Summertime Jud." That's the funny, pleasant Jud. He was always cracking jokes and fun to be around that time of year.

Tanya Webb didn't fare too well during our first year, and didn't get much playing time from Coach Gus as the season wore on. Whenever a guy's not playing and becomes disenchanted, he'll almost welcome a coaching a change, because it could mean better things for him with the new guy. When Tanya met Coach Heathcote for the first time, he immediately fell in love with him and talked about how much he liked Coach's personality. What he didn't know was that everybody loved Springtime/Summertime Jud Heathcote.

Once the season got going, Tanya and Coach butted heads more than anybody, and that was his last year playing MSU basketball.

# GULAG HEATHCOTE

Culture shock never abated that first season under Coach Heathcote. Practice wasn't fun, because everything was so structured. I'm sure some of that was due to the fact we still weren't winning. He lost his first three games as the Spartan coach, and then four of the first five. His initial win came against Eastern Michigan, and even then we needed overtime.

One thing Coach Heathcote did early on was to help me establish a confidence in myself by making me the main offensive weapon. He moved me back to my more natural forward slot so I didn't have to play center any more. As a result, I raised my scoring average 10 points, taking me from 11.7 points per game to 21.7 in a single season. After practice, Coach worked with me a lot with my outside shooting. I may not have liked the way he said things, or went about getting things done, or motivating us, but I always respected him because he was the person in authority.

Some guys, because they couldn't make that adjustment, didn't last. Milton Wiley, my freshman roommate—gone. Tanya Webb, after that first season—gone. Tanya transferred to Columbia Basin junior college in Washington. He then returned to MSU, but played defensive

When Jud Heathcote succeeded Gus Ganakas as the Spartan head coach, Michigan State immediately became one of the nation's leaders in sideline theatrics. Springtime/summertime Jud could, and would, make you laugh. Wintertime Jud could be very, um, dramatic. *Photo courtesy of Michigan State University*

tackle for the football team and got drafted in the 10th round by the New Orleans Saints in 1980.

I always felt that Coach Heathcote cared about us, but I also felt he came to Michigan State harboring certain untrue stereotypes that had been fed to him. We paid the price for that.

# A CLOUDED OUTLOOK

My military father helped me understand authority, discipline, and rules, which helped me with Coach Heathcote. I was also fortunate to have the support of my family, because sometimes I just couldn't take Coach's constant pounding. I had a car by then, and was so glad I could go home even if it was just for an evening meal with my parents. That allowed me to get away from it all, regroup, and come back for another round. If I had been hundreds of miles away, that wonderful outlet wouldn't have been an option, and I needed it, especially that year.

We finished 7-11 in the Big Ten and were 10-17 overall, although two losses to Minnesota were forfeited back to us after the Gophers were sanctioned by the NCAA. The losing and the transition from Coach Gus to Coach Heathcote made for very tough times. I needed the support of my folks. We knew we were better than our record, but even with Earvin and Jay coming in, there wasn't any reason for unbridled optimism.

I learned just how good a tactician Coach Heathcote was when we went down to Ann Arbor to play Michigan, who was ranked No. 3 in the country. The previous game, we had gotten got up and down really well, but all that week we practiced working the clock and shortening the game. Coach decided to slow the game down, and we were going to use the clock against Ricky Green and Phil Hubbard. We did that, and lo and behold, we not only stayed in the game, but we also gave ourselves an excellent chance to win.

I scored 25 points even playing that walk-it-up style. We missed a shot that could have won it at the end of regulation, and so did the Wolverines to send the game in overtime. They were highly ranked and playing a big rivalry game on their own floor, so you knew they were up for it, but we were right up there with them.

Ricky Green fleeced Terry Donnelly, our freshman point guard, twice near midcourt to take the ball in for easy baskets. We ended up losing by four points. However, we had taken the No. 3 team in the country to the limit in its own gym and came out saying to ourselves, "We're not that bad, just a little inexperienced and immature in certain areas."

Getting Earvin Johnson out of Everett High School in Lansing, Michigan, was key to fulfilling Michigan State's dream of a national championship. But landing his crosstown rival, Jay Vincent (No. 45), out of Lansing Eastern was just as important. Although the recruitment of Earvin got a little dicey, Jay was an easy sell. *Photo courtesy of Michigan State University*

We just didn't quite know how to finish or how to win. We knew we were better than our record, but certainly had no idea how good we'd be later on.

## DOWN FOR THE COUNT

The only game I ever missed in my Spartan career came at Illinois on the last day of the 1976-77 season. I woke up at 4:00 in the morning with unbelievable abdominal pain. I woke up my roommate, Ron Charles, and we called the trainer, Clint Thompson. Nothing he tried worked, so they took me to the hospital in Champaign where I spent the day. I listened to the game on the radio and the Spartans won, 62–61, when Edgar Wilson fittingly closed out his career with a basket at the buzzer.

I was able to go home the next day and it turned out I had something similar to an appendicitis attack, although I didn't have my appendix removed. However, a week later I had an allergic reaction to some of the medications the doctors gave me. I swelled up everywhere and broke out all over, which sent me back in the hospital for a couple more days.

It was a rough finish to a difficult season, but I felt that I had truly solidified my status as not only one of the best players in the Big Ten, but also as one of the better players in the country.

## "WE'VE GOT A PLAN"

When Vernon Payne and Gus Ganakas came down to Detroit to recruit me, they talked a lot about Earvin Johnson. The thing they'd always say to me is, "We've got a plan. If we can sign you, you'll be the start of it." They were moving beyond Terry Furlow because he was going to be a senior, and I think that Coach Ganakas had every intention to be at MSU throughout my career.

Vernon and Coach Ganakas said repeatedly that if they could sign me in '75, they were also going to go after Stuart House, a 6-foot-10, 230-pound center out of Detroit Denby High School who was going to be ranked the No. 1 or No. 2 player in the country. If they signed him and Earvin, the dazzling 6-foot-9 point guard at Lansing Everett High, they could almost guarantee a national championship before I graduated. Being 17 and naïve, I thought that sounded really good, because all I wanted to do was win. I often thought back to the Sukiran Bobcats and how we went 10-0. Winning just seemed like the thing to do, but I hadn't ever been able to capture that again—and this was seven years later.

Individually, I had a good freshman year at MSU. In the meantime, Coach Ganakas and Vernon were really going after Stuart, who was just a fantastic high school player. I remember going to one of his games in the state high school tournament. Denby was ranked among the top teams in the state but lost to Pontiac Central with this 10th grader named Walker D. Russell, who really turned it out. Walker was unbelievable and one of the best high school players I've ever seen.

I knew Stuart from playing AAU ball with him. He was a very outgoing guy on his own, but when his dad was around he became very quiet and reserved. His dad did all the talking and decision-making. When Stuart came to MSU for his visit, it seemed like Coach Ganakas and Vernon's plan was still on course.

When MSU fired Coach Ganakas, Stuart turned his interest—I should say Mr. House turned his interest—away from Michigan State. Stuart ended up signing with Washington State and George Raveling.

The funny thing is, in the summer of '77 I worked at Detroit Southwest Hospital, which was run by Ricky Ayala, who was the first African-American basketball player at Michigan State. Mr. House worked in the hospital's dispatch department, and I worked for him. By then, Stuart had already spent a year at Washington State but I'll never forget Mr. House telling me that Stuart was a lock for Michigan State until Coach Ganakas lost his job. They really could not buy into Jud Heathcote and felt no connection with him. That's what ultimately sealed Stuart's decision to go to WSU instead of MSU.

# A HOUSE UNITING

As a sophomore in 1976-77, I knew all about Earvin "Magic" Johnson. Who didn't? But then I started hearing a lot about a big man named Jay Vincent over at Lansing Eastern High School. While Earvin and Jay were being celebrated as cross-town rivals, Jud Heathcote was in his first year as the head coach at Michigan State. Coach Heathcote's Spartans took a back seat to Earvin's Vikings and Jay's Quakers in the Lansing area that season. A showdown between Earvin and Jay was even promoted with TV ads featuring both of them hamming it up.

Because neither of their high school gyms could accommodate the demand for tickets, administrators moved the game to MSU's 10,000-seat Jenison Field House. Jay's team won before a packed house that night, and it was the only time he had beaten Earvin in high school. I just remember watching Jay and thinking, "This guy's pretty good. He's got soft hands, he can catch, he can score, and he has deceptive quickness." He was kind of chubby because he still had some baby fat on him, but his moves were fluid. I recall thinking, "It sure would be nice if we could get both of them."

Every time we'd see Earvin we would tell him, "Hey man, you've gotta come to MSU, because we can be really good." Earvin was always around Jenison. He'd come to our games and be in the locker room afterwards. At that stage, I wouldn't say Earvin and I were friends, but we had developed a mutual admiration for each other.

He liked the way I played as a sophomore even though we weren't winning a lot of games and were drawing only about 5,000 fans. I think he could envision running the fast break with me and doing some special things in transition because I was a finisher and he was a great passer. I saw him as a guy who could deliver the basketball.

If he could make those cats he was playing with at Everett look as good as they did en route to winning a state championship, I knew he could help me and the team win. On the other hand, Jay never came around, but recruiting him was unbelievably easy.

# PIGS IN A BLANKET AND MILK

I like to tell people that Bob Chapman and I recruited Jay Vincent with three pigs in a blanket and two large glasses of milk. When he came for his official campus visit, we took him over to the IHOP restaurant on Grand River Avenue just east of campus.

Although it was Friday night, Jay ordered pigs in a blanket—you know, the little sausages wrapped in pancakes—and two large milks. When we walked into the restaurant, Jay was saying, "You guys are going to be pretty good next year." By the time we fed Jay and were ready to leave the IHOP, Jay was saying, "*We're* going to be good next year." We got Jay that night over an evening breakfast, or so we thought.

What we hadn't known was Jay was a homebody and not about to leave Lansing. He had been planning on coming to MSU all along.

# LANDING THE BIG ONE

There was a lot more acid indigestion involved with the recruitment of Earvin Johnson. Like everyone else, Earvin loved Gus Ganakas. With Coach Ganakas out of the picture after having been treated so poorly by MSU, the big worry was that Earvin would be less willing to take a chance with somebody he didn't know. Furthermore, word was getting out that Coach Heathcote was the antithesis of Coach Ganakas. After we lost Stuart House, there was definitely a concern that Earvin was going to go to the University of Michigan.

# A MAGICAL REVELATION

This is how I found out Earvin was going to sign. I got a phone call in my dorm room one evening and it was Vernon Payne on the other end. He used to call me "Big Fella," and he said, "Big Fella, how'd you like to play with Earvin Johnson next year?"

"Coach, you know I'd love nothing more than that," I said.

"Well, you're going to get your wish," he said. "You can't tell anybody, but he's going to sign tomorrow."

I look back on it, and Coach Ganakas and Vernon kept their promise. We didn't get Stuart House, but we got Earvin and Jay Vincent, who turned out to be one hell of a player and a perfect fit for us.

# VERNON PAYNE'S OBSCURE LEGACY

Vernon Payne remained at MSU for one season under Coach Heathcote, and then left to be the head coach at Wayne State University in Detroit. It was a fortuitous decision to retain Vernon, because I think he was the catalyst for getting Earvin's name on the dotted line. Vernon sold Earvin on the Spartans by saying you've got a solid nucleus with Bob Chapman and Greg Kelser, and Jud Heathcote *is a good coach.*

Vernon had to sell him on that, because Earvin wasn't used to somebody screaming and hollering and coaching from a negative

Vernon Payne, the Michigan State assistant coach who
discovered me while recruiting another player, doesn't get
nearly enough credit for laying the groundwork that
developed into the Spartans' first national championship.
*Photo courtesy of Michigan State University*

standpoint. Vernon doesn't get any credit for it, but he was unbelievably
important in signing Terry Donnelly, Ron Charles, Earvin Johnson,
and me.

After all, Michigan had been to the Final Four in 1975-76. The
Wolverines were ranked No. 1 most of the year in 1976-77, and they
made it to the regional final of the NCAA Tournament where they lost
to North Carolina-Charlotte. Michigan was a glamour program back
then, plus they had all these guys coming back. Phil Hubbard was an
All-American and an Olympian, so it would have been real easy for
Earvin to say, "I want to go there because I want to win, and if I join
that group, winning is not only going to come immediately, but it's
going to be at the highest level." Michigan State couldn't compare.

If Earvin joined Michigan at that time, it would have been once again Final-Four caliber. I was really, really worried he was going to go there. Johnny Orr, the Michigan head coach, and Bill Frieder, his chief assistant, were on him very strong. My anxiety was so bad I got to rationalizing that it wouldn't be so terrible if Earvin became a Wolverine. By that time we had Jay, and I said we're going to be a lot better with or without Earvin. You play those little games with yourself, so in case the disappointment comes you've kind of cushioned the blow, at least a little bit, ahead of time. I knew we'd still be good without him, but I also knew we had a chance to be great with him, and it would come right away.

The thing that helped get Earvin in the Spartan fold was the community. When he flew back home from some tournament he had played in, it seemed like the whole city was waiting at the airport to welcome him. These were Spartan fans, and they didn't want to lose him—especially to Michigan. So there was a lot of pressure for him to stay close to home.

I give Earvin a lot of credit because he could have gone to any program. But just as I had bought into what MSU was selling, which was an opportunity to be a part of something big down the road, Earvin did too.

In my opinion, his signing of Earvin was gift to the university on his way out the door. I liken it very much to the way Coach Ganakas convinced me to stay at MSU. Vernon could have easily said, "You shouldn't be at Michigan State" to both Earvin and me, and we would have left because we valued his word so much.

# 5

# THE ARRIVAL OF EARVIN JOHNSON AND COMING CLOSE IN 1977-78

## REALLY FAST FRIENDS

**G**oing into my junior year, I was the so-called big dog on the Michigan State basketball team, but that didn't mean a whole lot considering that the team was coming off a 12-15 record that included a couple of forfeits by Minnesota. I needed help. *We needed help*. It was never lost on me that basketball is a team game. I had scored points in high school and hadn't won. I had scored points my first two seasons at MSU and hadn't won. The amount of points I got meant very little to me. My best game as a sophomore was 33 points against the University of Detroit, and we had lost. I had 32 points at the University of Iowa, and we had lost. I averaged nearly 22 points a game as a sophomore, but we had lost more than we won. It wasn't about the points. I knew I could score on anybody. I wanted to win. So I welcomed this flashy freshman named Earvin "Magic" Johnson with open arms.

Now Earvin is smart, too. Just as after his collegiate career ended he went into Los Angeles saying "the Los Angeles Lakers are Kareem Abdul-Jabbar's team, and I'm just here to help him," he came into Michigan State as an 18-year-old with that same approach. He didn't try to take anything over. He didn't push anybody aside and say this is my team and all that.

Earvin was as respectful to me as he could be. We used to play in the summer quite a bit, and he would always talk about what "we" were going to do and how good "we" were going to be. He knew I was going to help him, and he knew he was going to help me. We knew Jay Vincent was going to help both of us, and we all knew we were going to have one helluva a fast break.

## EVERYTHING KEEPS FALLING INTO PLACE

I knew Earvin was a special player, and I could not wait to start playing alongside him. I had rejoiced when they brought the dunk back, and when we signed Earvin I had that same joy in me because I knew right then I was going to be able to win again. I was going to have a whole lot more fun, and that time between my sophomore and junior seasons took forever to go by.

Soon after Earvin signed his national letter-of-intent, he joined the pick-up games with us over at Jenison Field House. We'd have the college guys come in, and some pro guys would also show up. Terry Furlow would come back. George Gervin would come and play sometimes. That allowed us to start getting acquainted with each other's game, but seeing what he could do up close and in person ramped up my anticipation for the start of the season.

## 1977-78, THE TWO-YEAR MARCH TO THE NATIONAL TITLE BEGINS

Going into my junior season, I didn't know exactly how Coach Heathcote was going to use Earvin. Would Coach really truly give a freshman 6-foot-9 point guard the basketball and just let him run the show? I noted at the time that if Coach does that, then we're going to be a pretty tall team with Earvin in the backcourt and three legitimate front-line guys. Not only would the size work on our behalf, we'd be revolutionary because no one had ever seen a 6-foot-9 point guard before.

All my excitement and longing to play alongside Earvin in a Spartan uniform were building toward a crescendo when, just two days before the start of official practice, somebody fell into my left knee during a pickup game, causing me to sprain my medial collateral ligament.

# THE SPARTAN MILE

The good news about my injury was that I wouldn't have to run Coach Heathcote's stupid Spartan Mile, which was always held the day before the first practice. Guards had to cover the distance in five minutes and 30 seconds or under, forwards in 5:45, and the centers had to do it in six minutes. If you didn't meet your time, you had to do it over again. If you won it, you got your choice between a steak dinner with Coach or a pat on the back.

Who knows what Coach's diabolical reasons were, but I think it was his way of finding out who was in shape and who was willing to push themselves. There was always a lot of pressure on race day. Basketball doesn't really tie in all that well with distance running. Nevertheless, I would go all out and then practically collapse when I finished. My thinking was, if you've got to run it, you might as well try to win it.

I won the inaugural Spartan Mile as a sophomore with a time of 5:08 and accepted the pat on the back. I didn't want a steak dinner with Coach Heathcote. Can you imagine him and me alone at the table, and how one-sided that conversation would have been? I'm sure Coach would have given me an earful about everything I wasn't doing well in his estimation and I wouldn't have gotten a word in edgewise.

Venerable Jenison Fieldhouse sold out only when Michigan came to town in my first two seasons. After Earvin and Jay signed, the demand for tickets went through the roof of the old barn. *Photo courtesy of Michigan State University*

While I got out of running the Spartan Mile, I also had to further delay my official liftoff with Earvin, Jay, and our new look for four or five days.

## JUD'S WAY

When practice began, it was really hard to gauge how good we were going to be and how much fun we were going to have, because practice was so darn structured. We didn't get a lot of action up and down the court. We got a lot of up, whistle, stop; down, whistle, stop. Each time we stopped, Coach Heathcote would instruct, so to speak. We knew we were going to be a running team—flying through the open court and catching passes from Earvin, but we couldn't tell how effective we would be, because Coach was putting in a system and everything was so regimented.

Even so, we just knew it was going to happen.

# A NEW DAY

I told people before the season that we would be—and keep in mind I was 14-13 as a freshman and 12-15 as a sophomore—22 and 5. My prediction was for a whopping eight-game improvement over my best, but I just felt strongly that we weren't going to lose too many games at home. I thought we'd have maybe one loss in the non-conference portion of the schedule and maybe we'd have four losses in the Big Ten, which would mean we'd go 5-4 on the road and win all of our home games in the conference.

At the Big Ten Tipoff meetings in Chicago, each coach brings one or two players. Bob Chapman and I flew in with Coach Heathcote. At one point, we got into a little verbal sparring match with Mychal Thompson from Minnesota, who tried to tell us that the Gophers were going to kick our ass even though we had Earvin. Minnesota was going to be good because they had Kevin McHale, Ray Williams, and Mychal; but we told him it was a new day.

# THE FIRST GLIMPSE

Our first taste of real competition was in an exhibition game against the University of Windsor. The demand for season tickets was incredible, and they had to hold a lottery to make sure everybody got a fair chance. I remember walking through Jenison one day and hearing them read off the names of the lottery winners. The people who got them were so glad. It was funny because you couldn't give tickets away a year earlier.

Windsor was no match, but it gave us glimpse of what we had. We scored easily, we scored in transition—Earvin was dishing, and I was dunking. The house was packed for a meaningless game, and it was a beautiful thing because before that, the only time we'd fill the old barn was when Michigan came to town.

To see Jenison overflowing and to feel all that energy that Earvin brought was tremendous. That's why I didn't think we were going to lose any games at home. How are you going to lose when you've got that kind of support behind you?

# THE PROTOTYPICAL POINT FORWARD

Coach Heathcote started off playing Earvin in the frontcourt. Throughout the 62 games he played as a Spartan, Earvin was always in the frontcourt on defense, and then he would go get the ball and handle it on offense.

Now Coach had this thing for always wanting a 7-footer in the lineup. Jim Coutre was our 6-foot-9 center the year before, and at times he was a wild man. He flailed a lot, and when you threw the ball into Coutre, you hoped he'd catch it. He wasn't a finisher, but he played hard. He certainly wasn't in the caliber of Jay Vincent, and that was one of the reasons I was so happy we got Jay, because I knew that you could throw the ball inside and he would catch it. But Coach also recruited Sten Feldreich, a 7-footer from Sweden who was in that freshman class with Earvin and Jay.

Well, Coach tried to force Sten Feldreich in there, and he started him from day one. It was Earvin, Sten, and me on the front line, and Terry Donnelly and Bob Chapman in the backcourt. Don't let that fool you. Earvin was doing a lot of the ball-handling right from the start. It was as simple as that. When we'd be in our transition offense, the ball was in his hands. When we'd go into our halfcourt offense, and we were running our plays, Earvin would go to the forward position. His spot in Jud's high-low offense was out on the wing at times, or on the free-throw line at the high post. When we were in transition, it was straight-up Earvin right from the very beginning.

# A NOT-SO MAGICAL DEBUT

Central Michigan, who beat us up in Mount Pleasant the previous year in Coach Heathcote's very first game with Michigan State, came in for our season opener. This was Earvin's first real college game, and Jenison was packed. For the first time, Earvin was nervous and did not have a good game. He had seven points on 3-for-11 shooting, nine rebounds and eight assists, but he also had eight turnovers, and we were struggling.

That week in practice, Jay had just been annihilating people. I don't care who Coach had in there—Sten Feldreich; Les DeYoung, who was a left-handed post man; or the previous season's starting center Jim Coutre—Jay destroyed them all.

We couldn't seem to pull away from the Chippewas until Jay went in and just methodically took them apart. He got 25 points and six rebounds in 24 minutes. Jud's quote after the game was, "He saved us." If Jay hadn't come off the bench and done his thing, we would have lost to Central Michigan on our home floor in Earvin's debut. Coach Heathcote finally stopped trying to force Sten up front, and replaced him with Jay for the starting lineup from that point on.

# THE MAGICIAN MAKES DOUBT DISAPPEAR

Our next game was against Rhode Island in the Carrier Classic, hosted by Syracuse University in the Carrier Dome. We beat them, 92–64, and I had quietest 24 points I ever scored. I was getting precision passes from Earvin and scoring from point-blank range. It was fantastic.

We lost to Syracuse, 75–67, in the championship game even though the score was tied with a minute and a half to go. Earvin, however, displayed such an overwhelming personality and was so dynamic that he got the MVP award while playing for the second-place team in Syracuse's own tournament, which they won, in their own arena. That was one of only three non-conference games we would lose in Earvin's two seasons at MSU.

In our next game, Earvin got 20 rebounds at home against Wichita State. The headline in the next day's paper was Magic Reveals New Trick—20 Rebounds. That brought out the competitiveness in me. I wasn't jealous of my teammate, but I didn't want to get lost in Earvin's overwhelming shadow. I was telling everybody I was ecstatic that we were winning, but I didn't want to be just a bit player in the Magic Show.

Our next game was against Western Michigan, and I made a decision. I had the 27 rebounds against Wisconsin as a freshman, but I said, "I'm going to get 20 rebounds against Western today." The

Broncos had beaten us the previous year, too, and that was in Jenison. So we jumped on Western early and at halftime I had 21 points and 11 rebounds. I didn't care about the points; I said to myself, "I'm going to get those rebounds."

Well, we were winning handily in the second half, and Coach Heathcote pulled us back. We stopped running and pressing and were working the ball. I played about 10 more minutes and only got three more rebounds, so I didn't get my 20 rebounds, but I would have had he left me in.

I was asked in the locker room afterward if I resented all the recognition and publicity that Earvin was getting in light of the fact my 25-point, 14-rebound performance could go unnoticed? And I said, "no, because last year at this time we were 1-4 and now we're 4-1. If we keep winning, we'll all get our due credit."

# SHOWDOWN IN MOTOWN STARRING DICK VITALE, AS HIMSELF

After beating Middle Tennessee State we made the big road trip to the University of Detroit on December 21, 1977. It's one of those games I will never forget.

The previous season, long before Dick Vitale found fame and fortune as a college basketball analyst for ESPN, he coached U of D to its first NCAA Tournament appearance in 15 years and only the second in school history. The Titans lost to Michigan in the second round but played really well. That was Vitale's final game on the bench, but he became the school's athletic director and named his assistant, Smokey Gaines, to replace him as head coach.

We were playing the Titans in their arena, Calihan Hall. They were 5-0 and ranked 15th. It was a greatly anticipated matchup, and we were a little bit nervous going in. They were coming off a 24-win season and had Terry Tyler, John Long, Terry Duerod, and Kevin Smith from the team that defeated us the year before, 99–94, in East Lansing. They also beat us my freshman year in Detroit's Cobo Hall despite Terry Furlow's 41-point effort.

Even though it was a snowy night, the game drew a huge crowd. There was very little room for MSU fans, and they put those who got tickets up near the ceiling. This was a City game for real bragging rights because everybody on both teams knew each other.

Before the game, something amazing—which is now commonplace for college basketball fans—happened. Vitale came out onto the floor to fire up the crowd even more than it already was. While the two teams were warming up, Vitale took the microphone and screamed, "I want to hear you guys all night. We're going to show the Magic Man that there will be no magic here in Calihan Hall tonight, bay-beeee!"

He was already into his shtick, but what was even crazier was that he did the game on television. Channel 2 carried it locally and he was the guest analyst. He was being Dickie V before there was Dickie V. That's where all that emanated from. He was a fiery, wild, crazy guy and already had the slang down. No coach or athletic director that I'm aware of had ever done that before.

After they introduced us, they turned the lights down and with the pyrotechnics as they were in 1977, introduced the Titans to an unbelievable fireworks show. It took 10 minutes. They introduced all the reserves and then the starting line up, and we just sat there watching.

It was a tight game early, but then we started to pull away and were wowing their crowd with Earvin's passing and my scoring. I had 20 points at halftime, and we were up by seven. In the second half, I came to truly appreciate Coach Heathcote's coaching acumen for the very first time because we had scouted them so well, we knew how to take them out of what they wanted to do and defended them extraordinarily well. We ran our offense and executed it like we never had before, and they couldn't deal with it.

We eventually pulled so far away, that with about 15 minutes to go, the U of D crowd started cheering for us. We ended up drilling them 103–74—a 29-point victory on their floor—and if we had kept pounding we could have gotten 120. That night, I felt like I could score 50, but we went to our spread offense with seven minutes to go, and I ended up with 36 and 10 boards. I was doing whatever I wanted to do, Bob Chapman had 22 points and Earvin got the first triple-double of his career with 11 points, 10 rebounds, and 13 assists.

The headline in the next morning's Detroit Free Press bellowed BIG GAME JUST A BIG ROUT! MSU CREAMS U-D, 103–74.

That's when I really knew we had a good team. If "Who's Your Daddy?" had been popular back then, we would have probably been chanting that, because we commandeered their building and their fans.

# BACK TO REALITY

After beating Detroit, we were going to have four or five days off for Christmas break before going to Norfolk, Virginia, to play in the Old Dominion Classic. I was going to stay in Detroit, and Ron Charles was going to stay at my house so I could drive him to the airport the next morning for his flight back home to the Virgin Islands.

We had two managers on that team, Dean Thedos and Darwin Payton. Darwin was staying behind because he was from River Rouge, but everybody else who didn't have alternate plans—like Dean—was supposed to ride the team bus back to East Lansing. I guess in all the exhilaration and exuberance from the win, the bus left without Dean.

Quite naturally, I wanted to celebrate. I had friends at the game and I wanted to have a good time with them, but Dean begged me to take him back to school. And I'm like, "Dean, man, you've got to be joking." But I ended up taking him back in a driving snowstorm with Ron Charles. It took us two and a half hours to get there and probably two and half to get back.

So my big night—career-high 36 points, finally beating U of D—was celebrated how? By taking Dean Thedos back to East Lansing in a snowstorm.

I suffered a cut over the eye when I got hit with an elbow and played most of the game with a Band-Aid, which I still had on the next day when I went shopping at the mall. Everybody had seen the game, and needless to say I enjoyed being quite the celebrity in the City of Detroit.

I remember those times every time I see the scar just below my left eyebrow.

# THE 75 OFFENSE

When we'd get a comfortable lead, and with no 35-second shot clock in play back then, Coach Heathcote would take the air out of the ball. It was called our 75 Offense, which means you only took a shot if you had a 75-percent chance of making it. He'd force the opponent to foul us, and then we'd make free throws.

What shots are 75-percent sure?

Lay-ups!

So that's what we would work the ball around to get.

# LET THE GOOD TIMES ROLL

We beat SMU and New Hampshire to win the Old Dominion Classic and we were winning. This was all new to me because I hadn't won like this in a long time, but I liked it. We went 8-1 in the non-conference and then won our first seven games in the Big Ten. We were 15-1, and won 13 straight games after the Syracuse loss. By that time we had cracked the Top 10 and were ranked seventh in the country.

Our seventh Big Ten victory came at Ohio State. We were supposed to play on Thursday, but we got hit with a snowstorm and the game was postponed. We spent two extra days in Columbus, and the game ended up being played on Saturday instead.

After beating the Buckeyes, we went back to our hotel, the Holiday Inn on Lane Avenue right across the street from St. John Arena. We had a curfew, but there was this real nice party going on downstairs. We got in our rooms for bed check, but we had already decided to go to that party. We got down there, and at about one o'clock in the morning, we spotted Don Monson, one of the assistant coaches, in the lobby. He peeked his head into the party, and you should have seen all of us crawling on the floor. It was funny because the ladies we were dancing with and who were celebrating us as big heroes for winning the basketball game, were laughing at us trying to avoid being seen.

We made it to a service elevator, which we were planning to take to our rooms on the sixth floor. However, somebody hit the button for the fifth floor, where the coaches were staying. Everybody believed it to be Ron Charles because he seemed to be especially nervous. Someone quickly pushed the fourth floor so we could get out there and take the staircase up two flights. The last thing we wanted was to have the doors open with all of us in the elevator on Coach Heathcote's floor—heck no!

# UNDAUNTED BY DEFEAT

We were 7-0 in the Big Ten and ranked No. 7 in the country. The game we were supposed to play at Indiana on Saturday also got moved back, and we had already been on the road for a while. We went to Bloomington on Sunday and practiced there and then played the Hoosiers on Monday night. We lost by 5, but weren't all that disappointed. They played better than we did, and we still had a chance to win, so we weren't crushed by it. We had won 13 games and only lost one on the road.

# DAMNED WOLVERINES

We were looking forward to getting back home—me especially so—because our next game was against Michigan. I was 0-4 against the Wolverines, having lost two games in overtime to them in Ann Arbor, and two in regulation in East Lansing. In each instance, they were the better team, but this time we were undoubtedly superior. I was looking forward to finally beating Michigan.

Johnny Orr brought his team in for the Thursday night game without All-American Phil Hubbard, who had had season-ending knee surgery. They were still a good team, but not as good as we were. I got so sky-high for that game it must have affected me negatively, because I ended up with 10 points and only one rebound, and I was in foul trouble.

Earvin, Jay, Ron, Terry, and Bob did all they could to keep us in it, but we seemed to be fighting from behind the whole time. We finally got the game tied and they had the ball, but Earvin stole it and kicked it out to Bob Chapman with under a minute left. Bob went up for a lay-up, but Dave Baxter blocked his shot. I got really angry because I thought Bob should have gone up for a dunk and at least gotten fouled. By laying it up, he allowed Baxter to pin the ball against the backboard. They got the ball back, and seldom-used Mark Lozier made a shot from the top of the key at the buzzer to beat us 65–63.

What stands out most about that game was Johnny Orr running across the court and blowing kisses to the MSU student cheering section.

That was the most crushing defeat of my college career because Michigan is our acknowledged rival and nemesis. I couldn't beat them when they were better, but we came close, and now we were finally better and we still didn't win. You hear coaches and players talk about finding it difficult to pick yourself up after an especially tough defeat, and I felt it first-hand. I almost felt like I didn't want to play basketball anymore. That loss had that type of impact on me. It was a horrifying defeat. It sent all kinds of messages my way—you think you're good, but you're still not good enough. And then to see Johnny Orr blow kisses the way he did made it especially difficult.

The next day while watching film, Coach Heathcote didn't make it any better because what did he do? When he got to my one rebound he just kept playing it back over and over. I'd get the rebound, and he'd rewind it; I'd get the rebound, and he'd rewind it; I'd get the rebound, and he'd rewind it. "I want you to look at this, because it's the only one you got all night," he said. "We could always count on you to rebound." He replayed it at least 15 times. There was no winning with Coach.

## THE REMATCH

We lost two straight and fell back into a tie for first place, but we got back on the winning track by beating Indiana and Iowa, and then we got Michigan again, in Ann Arbor. This time, I intentionally kept myself low. I played a psychological mind game with myself and refused to get jacked up. I convinced myself it was just another game. I wasn't looking forward to it and didn't get excited about it one bit. It was no big deal and I kept it that way. I did that because I don't know how I would have gotten by another loss to Michigan. In effect, I prepared myself for the worst, and if we lose, fine we lose. At least I wouldn't be falling from such a high emotional peak. I intentionally kept myself on an even keel.

We went into Crisler Arena, where I never had a bad individual game. I had 22 points, 10 rebounds, and a couple of blocked shots including one against Mr. Lozier, who hit the basket to beat us in the previous game. He got into my side of the zone, went up for a jumper, and I slapped it up into the crowd. He didn't score a point in that game and we won by 11.

When it was over, I felt nothing. I felt cheated, because I had been waiting to beat Michigan for so long, but because I had not allowed myself to get up, I was left with an empty feeling. It felt no different than beating Central Michigan or Western Michigan.

I remember reading about Jerry West, who had lost to the Boston Celtics for so many years when he was with the Los Angeles Lakers. He felt at times like not playing anymore and just wanting to quit because at some point you come to the realization that maybe the other guys are better, and you're not good enough. And after all those disappointments, when he finally won his one NBA championship as a player in 1972, it rang hollow for him because it was like, is this all there is?

So after finally getting a victory in my sixth try against Michigan, it was like, "Is that it?" I knew exactly where Jerry West was coming from. I got nothing out of that win, other than the fact that it was important to our goal of having a really good season.

# KNOCKED OUT BY LEON SPINKS

Our only other loss of the regular season came on February 16, 1978, at Purdue by the score of 99–80 and I blame it on Leon Spinks. The night before that game, we were watching the first heavyweight fight between Spinks and Muhammad Ali. We were all big Ali fans, and the only one rooting for Spinks was Terry Donnelly because Spinks was from St. Louis and so was Terry.

Spinks pulled the upset that night, and except for Terry, we were really disappointed. It obviously lingered because we had nothing for the Boilermakers. They jumped on us early and never got off. We had a chance to win each of the other three games we lost, but we didn't have a chance in that one. The only thing that was in doubt was whether they'd get 100.

# THE SINGING SPARTANS

On the way home that night after losing miserably to the Boilermakers Earvin, Jay, Ron, Bob and I were all in the back of the bus playing music. Since we had just got whupped, Coach Heathcote didn't want any music going on.

He hollered back to us, "Cut the damn music off."

For whatever reason, something got into all of us. We turned the music off, but then we started singing.

So then Coach yelled, "I don't want any singing coming from back there either," with a few expletives thrown in for good measure.

Since he didn't want to hear singing, and it was about midnight, and we just got our butts kicked, we were as angry as he was and not happy about it. But that night, as a group, we just decided to be defiant. And since he didn't want to hear any singing, we started humming.

So he sent Don Monson back to us and he said, "A word to the wise, you may want to just cut it out."

After Mons left, I started reciting Martin Luther King Jr.'s "I Have a Dream" speech.

The next day in East Lansing, sure enough, Jud called a meeting, and everybody gathered in the tiny coaches' locker room in the basement of Jenison Field House. "Anybody in this room who thinks he's tougher than me," Coach said, "stand up right now."

Nobody stood up. The he said, "What happened last night will not happen again—ever. I'm telling you that right now. And if any of you think you're tougher than me, stand up."

We decided not to challenge him. We made our stand and said okay, that's it, leave it alone. Then we went and practiced. We were a pretty strong-minded group and sometimes we felt we at least needed to assert ourselves and serve a reminder that if 18 is the legal age, then we're grown men.

Of course, we never hummed again. You don't go to that well more than once.

# AN 11-YEAR TITLE DROUGHT ENDS

With two games to go, we went into Wisconsin with a chance to clinch the outright championship. We played really well and won. I had a really good game, and we cut the nets down from the Badgers' baskets. It was the only win I ever had at Wisconsin.

Our final regular-season game was at Minnesota. Earlier in the season it was thought that it would be for the Big Ten championship, but the Gophers had stumbled, and we had a two-game lead on them, so our game against them was meaningless.

The night before that game, there was no curfew, and we stayed up partying until four in the morning before a noon game. We thought that since we didn't need the game, Coach Heathcote would let up on the throttle a little bit. Wrong! He pushed harder than he ever did in that game. We wanted to win it, but we knew it wasn't vital, so we didn't put a whole lot of emphasis on it.

But with Coach pushing, we beat them on their home floor. It was Mychal Thompson and Ray Williams' last home game. We finished the regular season 15-3 in the Big Ten all alone in first place and 23-4, one game better than my 22-5 prediction. It was Michigan State's first championship since 1967, and the Spartans were heading for the NCAA Tournament for the first time in 19 years.

# YOUNG AND FOOLISH

We didn't know if we had what it took to be a national title contender, but I thought one thing that was going to be a huge advantage for us was the fact that we were going to be facing teams that didn't know us. With the exception of Syracuse—we would have killed the Orange on a neutral floor, let alone at Jenison—the non-conference teams we faced couldn't handle us. They didn't know how to deal with our size, and they didn't know what to do with Earvin handling the ball. I felt we had a legitimate shot to get to the Final Four.

We looked at the bracket and saw Kentucky, which was ranked No. 1 all year long, probably waiting for us in the Regional final because the Wildcats were a very experienced, senior-laden team. But we felt we could beat them. I remember Coach Heathcote telling the crowd that met us at the airport when we got back from our game in Minnesota that we're young and maybe ahead of schedule, but we might be foolish enough to think we can win this thing. Hearing him say that gave us confidence because he was one who would always take a path of cautiousness and not be too optimistic in his appraisal of what we were capable of doing.

# EASY PICKINGS

We opened against Providence in Indianapolis, and they were a good team but no match for us. We were staying in the same hotel as the New York Knicks, who played the Indiana Pacers the night before our game. Ron Charles, my roommate, and I ran into Knicks head coach and former playing great Willis Reed in the hallway. He talked to us and was really friendly. Ron told him he had attended one of his basketball camps in New York years back and Willis said he remembered him, although he might have just been saying that. But he was very nice and Willis was one of my childhood heroes. I remember being inspired by him after Bill Russell retired from the Boston Celtics, and the Knicks became my favorite team. Willis was the MVP of the league, the All-Star game, and the Finals in 1970, so meeting him was a thrill. Then we met Bob McAdoo, who was playing for the Knicks, and who later would be my teammate in the NBA.

Marquette was the defending national champion, and they lost to Miami of Ohio prior to our game against Providence. We were waiting to take the court as they were coming off, and I'll never forget the look on the faces of Jerome Whitehead and Butch Lee. They were stunned, and I remember thinking, "I don't want to be like that." So we handled Providence. During the game, I remember Dan Roundfield, who was playing for the Pacers at that time and I knew from Detroit, sitting in the MSU cheering section at Market Square Arena. It was fun meeting those pro athletes and having my parents and family there.

Our next game was in Dayton against Western Kentucky, who won its first-round game against Syracuse in overtime. We beat the Hilltoppers with ease, and that set up our game against Kentucky.

# LESSONS LEARNED

Kentucky had all this experience. The Wildcats had Rick Robey, who would be taken by Boston with the No. 3 overall pick in the NBA draft; Mike Phillips, who was a big, burly center; Jack Givens, who would later score 41 points in the championship against Duke and was a first-round pick of the Atlanta Hawks; and Kyle Macy, who would later become a first-round pick of the Phoenix Suns in 1979 after staying at Kentucky for a fifth year. Even so, when that game started, we realized early on that we could beat them. They had all sorts of problems with our matchup zone and couldn't get the ball inside. We, on the other hand, were able to operate our halfcourt offense and do some things we wanted to do with regard to getting the ball into the post.

What we weren't able to do is run our fast break much on them, but I think that was a byproduct of our conservative strategy rather than what the Wildcats were doing to stop us. I think Coach later acknowledged that we should have gone after them like we went after everybody else. We should have just gone all-out, pushing the ball and not looking to slow the tempo. That was a miscalculation because slowing that game down helped them, not us. We should not have been fearful of running against them.

We had a five-point lead at halftime and scored the first basket of the second half to go up by seven. We knew Kentucky was never really out of it, but usually we could hold a seven-point lead. Unfortunately, that was Earvin's second poor game of the year and first since the opener against Central Michigan. He made only two of 10 shots, scored six points, had four rebounds, turned the ball over and had foul difficulty. He could never really get going, and I think part of the reason he struggled was our conservative approach.

We were playing halfcourt, passing it around, trying to get the highest percentage shot and ended up scoring 49 points to Kentucky's 52. Near the end of the game, the lead kept bouncing back and forth from one to three. We didn't have the three-point shot and we had to foul, so we kept putting Kyle Macy on the line, and he kept making free throws.

The 1977-78 Big Ten champion Spartans might have gone on to win the national title that season had we not abandoned our up-tempo game in favor of a more deliberate attack against Kentucky in the NCAA Tournament regional final in Dayton. I scored a game-high 19 points, but it wasn't enough to get MSU into the Final Four. We lost to the Wildcats by the score of 52–49 after netting 60 points or more in each of our previous 29 games and 80 or more 11 times. *Photo courtesy of Michigan State University*

If you had told me before the game that we'd hold Kentucky to 52 points and lose, I would not have believed it. If you had told me we would score just 49, I wouldn't have believed that. We got 49 in a half against some teams. It was on March 18, my dad's birthday, and he was there with my mom. It was our fault that we lost to the Wildcats.

Afterward, I tried to be a gentleman and a sportsman and congratulated the Wildcats. And as we were leaving, I even went to their team bus and wished them the best of luck for the next week in St. Louis for the Final Four.

It was a lesson for everybody, the coach and players. I watched the national semifinals the following week. Kentucky beat Arkansas with Sidney Moncrief; and I watched Duke, with Mike Gminski, Jim Spanarkle, and Gene Banks, beat Notre Dame. But I couldn't bring myself to watch much of the championship game, because Kentucky did not look all that impressive to me against Arkansas, and I couldn't help but think, "Man, we should be there."

Goose Givens, who had 14 points against us, tore Duke apart with 41, and I became even more depressed. What it did was make us realize what we were going to have the following season. We were graduating some seniors, but Bob Chapman was the only starter we were losing. And we said to ourselves, "If we improve at all, how can we not win the national championship?"

# 6

# NEARLY LOSING IT ALL

## ALL THE WAY WITH SPECIAL K

Just like "Butch Cassidy and the Sundance Kid," "Magic and Special K" had a ring to it. However, the most recognized tandem in Michigan State history wasn't the creation of some PR guy. Earvin Johnson got his nickname in high school, while I was christened during my junior year at MSU.

Someone started calling me "Dr. K" when I was at Detroit Henry Ford High. I didn't like it because it was a play on "Dr. J," and no one could come close to Julius Erving. The Special K thing came about a few years later at MSU. I want to say that Darwin Payton, one of our team managers, started it. Then it was in the paper one day, and once that happens—boom!

## THIS COULD BE THE YEAR FOR MSU, DUKE, NOTRE DAME . . .

After we lost to Kentucky in the 1978 regional final and then the Wildcats went on to win the whole thing the following week, we were beside ourselves thinking, "It should have been us." We were just as good, if not better than they were. We got beat despite giving up just 52 points. Our team was supposed to win that kind of game by 20, so how was it we only scored 49 points?

Since we only lost one starter—Bob Chapman—from that team, we felt very strongly about our chances in 1978-79. But Duke, which lost to Kentucky in the championship game, also had most of its team coming back. Notre Dame was returning everybody from its Final Four team. Kansas and Cal-State Fullerton, which like us were Elite Eight teams, also had everyone coming back. We were in there with a bunch of teams that felt it could be their year. It was going to be a matter of seeing who could make it a reality.

## BRAZIL '78

During the off-season, I got a call from Coach Heathcote about whether I was interested in going to Brazil to play in a tournament. We'd be gone for almost two weeks, and we were going only if Earvin and I were up for it. I wasn't surprised Coach deferred to us, because he was big on seniority and we could only take 10 guys, which meant the incoming freshmen couldn't come along. Furthermore, we'd have to gather in East Lansing to practice in early September. If we said yes, summer vacation would be over because school would be in session when we returned.

We jumped at the opportunity because we felt it would kick-start what we wanted to do. We didn't think about how long it would make the season and the fatigue that might ensue. When you're young like that, you just want to play, and the more you play against other competition the better. We all showed up, they put us in the dorms, we practiced about a week and we left.

## TEAM USA

The thing that was really neat and came as a complete surprise was that when we got to Brazil we were no longer Michigan State—we were the United States. We wore red, white, and blue uniforms with "USA" stitched on the front. Since it was an international competition, the only numbers allowed were 1 through 15, so only a couple guys could wear their real numbers. Mike Brkovich could wear No. 12. Instead of No. 32, I wore No. 10.

The other three teams were Uruguay, Argentina, and Brazil—the strongest team with the sensational Oscar Schmidt and a bunch of other professional players.

# A BONDING PROCESS

We couldn't drink the water or eat any of the local snacks. We only drank bottled water and soft drinks, and all our food was brought in. It was the only time Earvin and I were roommates on the road. Coach Heathcote had assigned Jay Vincent to me for the rest of the year because he wanted me to rub off on him; and he assigned Earvin to Bobo Charles because he wanted him to rub off on Ron. It made sense because why would you want your two captains rooming together when they could be influencing other players?

# EASY COME, EASY GO

One morning, Darwin Payton went down to the front desk at our hotel to exchange a ten-dollar bill for Brazilian currency, which at that time was Cruzeiros. They inadvertently gave him the equivalent of $100 American. Darwin was so happy that he bought everybody gifts from the street vendors.

Later that same day, Mike Longaker, our scholar-athlete and 4.0 student, went down and they did the same thing. Now if this happened today, as an adult you'd point out the person's mistake and give the overage back. But as an 18- or 19-year-old kid who doesn't have any money, that's like a bonus. You're not giving that back. Well, instead of leaving well enough alone, Longaker went back down there with another $10 bill, except this time the desk people caught their mistake. To make matters worse, they realized that it happened two other times and wanted all their money back.

By that time, Darwin had spent most of his, and Coach Heathcote didn't make him give it back. But Longaker had to return all of it because as Coach put it, it was stupid to try to capitalize a second time. We busted on our resident genius about that the rest of the trip.

The march to March began for the 1978-79 Spartans in September with a preseason tournament in Brazil as Team USA. Representing the United States was a thrill none of us will ever forget, and beating older, more experienced players gave us the confidence we could defeat any college team back in the States. *Photo courtesy of Michigan State University*

# WINNING, LOSING, AND LEARNING

On September 17, 1978, I turned 21 years old in beautiful Rio de Janeiro. We didn't make that big a deal about it, but Coach Heathcote did give me a leather cowboy hat. You could get all sorts of things from the street vendors. I guess he wanted me to be a gaucho.

There were two round-robin tournaments, the first of which was in Rio. We beat Uruguay and Argentina handily, and so did Brazil, who we ended up meeting in the final. It was a great game for a while, but just before halftime, I got hit in the knee and it buckled. We were leading by four, but I was done. We got blown out in the second half, and on the bus back to the hotel I remember Earvin saying, "I see now that we better not get anybody hurt this season," because it all came apart.

What went through my mind was the year before when Michigan went on a basketball tour in Europe and Phil Hubbard tore his knee up. He missed the entire season after undergoing surgery. All I could think was, "Am I going to need surgery? Am I going to miss the season?"

We had three days off before playing the second mini-tournament in Sao Paulo, and during that time, I underwent rigorous treatment. It turned out to be just a sprained medial collateral ligament—thank goodness there was no tear. I wore a brace and played sparingly against Uruguay, but didn't wear the brace when we beat Argentina.

Then we had the big gold-medal matchup against Brazil, and it was an unbelievable game. We won in double-overtime and I had 27 points, Earvin had 25, and Oscar Schmidt had something like 30, but it would have been a lot more if there had been a three-point line.

## BRINGING HOME A MEDAL AND AN ATTITUDE

I still have the medal; it's somewhere at my mom's house. We were really proud after beating Brazil because we felt if we could beat a seasoned team like that, we should be OK against college guys back in the States. Coach only knows one way to go, and he coached that Brazil situation like it was the Big Ten season. It was a tremendous growing experience, as well. The one big difference was we didn't have a curfew. Coach trusted us to do the right thing, and we did whatever we wanted in groups. It was kind of unusual seeing 10 guys, with four or five of us 6-foot-7 or taller, walking down the street while we were sightseeing or going to a show. We kept our priorities. We knew what we were there for and accomplished our goal. We had a great time in South America, and winning the tournament was tremendous, but we were ready to go home. Today's coaches complain about long seasons and fatigue, but we thought that month together put us ahead of everybody else in the nation.

## A HIGHLY COMPETITIVE ENVIRONMENT

When we got back from Brazil, school had already been in session for about a week. Our prize freshman in 1978-79 was Rob Gonzalez from Detroit Catholic Central High School, and in our absence he had made it known around campus that he was the new man on the block. He had been playing really well in pick-up games at Jenison and was serving notice that when the guys got back, he'll stake his claim on playing time. He was a real cocksure, confident kind of guy.

When we got back in town, Coach Heathcote told us to take a few days off and not rush back to the gym, because we had been playing for almost a month. We laid low for one day, but when Earvin heard about all this trash Gonzalez had been talking, he said he was going to play. I decided to take another day off to rest my knee because those pick-up games were hard-fought, and crowds of about 200 people came to watch them.

Earvin and I decorated the Spartan—the campus icon known as "Sparty"—with our Big Ten championship trophy (right) and the one we won in Brazil (left), but we went into the 1978-79 season wanting more. And we got it. *Photo courtesy of Michigan State University*

Earvin made Rob Gonzalez his personal assignment. He was talking to Rob, and dogging him, and berating him—in a competitive way—and beat him so bad in front of all those people it was embarrassing. I still playfully blame Earvin for Rob's demise that season because he destroyed Rob and took away his confidence that day. He let him know that, "No, you're not going to walk in here and take over anything."

# THE RUSSIANS ARE COMING, AND GOING DOWN

The Soviet Union national team kicked the butt of every college team they played during the exhibition season. They beat Oregon State, Arkansas, Notre Dame, and some other good college teams, so we felt if we could beat them that we really were on to something.

They came in with all of their size, experience, international success, and tons of credit for gaining on the U.S. in terms of basketball prowess. Plus, they were being touted as one of the favorites in the 1980 Olympics. These were grown men, not 18-, 19-, 20-year-old kids like we were. But when that game began, it was clear they could not handle our speed and athleticism. I jumped center against Vladamir Tkachenko, who's 7-foot-3, and won it easily. He was a big joker, but I was on my way down before he got off the floor.

We jumped on top them so quickly it was incredible. Earvin had 13 points, 13 assists, seven rebounds, and five steals. I scored 24 points, had 10 rebounds, six steals, and three blocks—that's a pretty nice line right there. Coach Heathcote referred to me as, "Sometimes Spiderman and sometimes spaceman." We outran and outrebounded them and won both halves by identical 38–30 scores. The final was 76–60 and when that game was over, we thought we had separated ourselves from the rest of the competition.

# THE LURKING IRISH

Notre Dame wasn't on our schedule, but we sure saw the Fighting Irish a lot. It seemed like they were on TV all the time. I remember that after they lost their national semifinal game to Duke a year earlier, Kelly

Tripucka, who was a freshman that year, said that without a doubt the Irish would win a championship before he left. Who could blame him for thinking that? After all, they had a very young team and had just gotten to the Final Four.

We didn't know if we would be seeing them down the road, but we were very aware of Notre Dame and even envious in a way. It was probably like a lot of teams are with Duke nowadays. You want what they have.

## WEARING THE BULL'S-EYE

After beating Central Michigan in the opener, we hosted Cal State–Fullerton, who had made it to the Elite Eight the previous season. Those guys really gave us game. They were trash-talking and looked at us like we looked at Notre Dame. They wanted a piece of Michigan State with Earvin "Magic" Johnson and Special K. They wanted to show the nation they were just as good if not better. We only won 92–89, and Coach Heathcote was very upset afterward because although they couldn't stop us, we couldn't stop them, and he's a defensive-minded guy. He let us know he didn't take very kindly to someone scoring that many points on our home floor, so that's all we worked on in practice for the next few days.

## A BIGGER STAGE

An easy win at Western Michigan set up our trip Chapel Hill, North Carolina, to visit UNC. A promising prospect by the name of James Worthy was being recruited hard by both schools, and he was at the game to see the Spartans and Tar Heels from close range. We went in wanting to stay within reach so they couldn't go into Coach Dean Smith's legendary four-corner offense and stall the ball out on us. The shot clock hadn't yet been introduced to the college game, and we knew if they got up by 10, they would go into the four corners and just eat time.

Of course, we fell behind by 9 or 10, and the Tar Heels went into it. Nevertheless, we were probably the only team that could forge a comeback against them after they spread it out. We really pressured up and forced them to put it on the floor, causing some turnovers. We got back into the game so well that we got to within one point and had the ball with 10 seconds to go. We passed inside to Jay Vincent, who took a shot from right in front of the basket at the buzzer, but it hit the back of the rim, rattled around, and bounced out. We lost by one and realized going undefeated just went out the door. Oh well.

# WHEN SMOKE GOT IN OUR EYES

We played Cincinnati before 31,683 fans in the first college game ever in the Pontiac Silverdome. At that time, it was the largest crowd ever for a basketball game in Michigan, and second-largest crowd nationally behind the Houston-UCLA game at the Astrodome in '68.

Coach got us off on a sour note in that one. We got a scouting report on each Bearcat player and the team's tendencies, and we went through all of it against our scouting team. But for the first and only time, Coach Heathcote decided to pull a little pop quiz in the locker room before the game. He started asking us specific questions about what was in the scouting report and names of Cincinnati players. None of us could answer, because quite frankly, we hadn't paid much attention to the scouting report.

Well, that ticked him off. Coach wasn't too good at concealing his anger, and he let us have it right then and there before we had to play the Bearcats. The thing I remember most about playing in the Silverdome was how smoky it was because smoking was still allowed inside. We played in a haze, literally and figuratively, because while we won by nine, we didn't put on a show. We didn't give those 31,863 folks the best that we had to offer.

# YOU CAN GO HOME AGAIN

Coach Heathcote took us to the Far West Classic in the Great Northwest, which is where he's from. The tournament, played in Portland, Oregon, featured eight teams including Washington State, where Coach Heathcote had played basketball and served as an assistant under his mentor, former Cougar coach Marv Harshman; Washington,

It became evident Michigan State wasn't going to sneak up on anybody early in the 1978-79 season. Cal State-Fullerton, which had made it to the Elite Eight the previous season, came to East Lansing hoping to quiet all the talk about Earvin "Magic" Johnson and the Spartans, and almost did. We had the makings of a great defensive team with (l-r) Ron Charles, Jay Vincent, me (hidden in the background), and Earvin. But we weren't very good on the defensive end that day and won by only three points, 92-89.
*Photo courtesy of Michigan State University*

where he got his master's degree and Harshman was the current coach; and Indiana with Coach Bobby Knight.

Coach Heathcote wanted to win badly and look good doing it in front of his home folks. We wanted it for him. We were ranked No. 4 in the nation and faced Washington State, which was 7-0 and coming off a win at Ohio State, in the opener. Stuart House, who Michigan State had lost in recruiting after Coach Heathcote was hired, was the Cougars' power forward, and they had Don Collins, an eventual first-round draft pick of the Atlanta Hawks. They had a good team, but we got out to a 21–6 start, and later in the first half used a 15–0 run to go ahead 46–17. Game over. We dispatched them 98–52, and Coach was happy.

The next day we played a good Oregon State team with Steve Johnson, who would go as a first-round pick to the Kansas City Kings, and it was a dogfight. They were good and playing at home. We went in at halftime with a small lead, thinking we were going to get chewed out, and Coach said, "Guys, that's a pretty good team we're playing out there, aren't they?" He was absolutely right, but that never mattered before when we couldn't get it done against a *pretty good team*. It was always something we weren't doing. You just never knew where he was coming from.

The funny thing about that game was, after intermission, we were greeted outside of our locker room by Bobby Knight. He was patting us on the back and saying, "C'mon boys, let's go get 'em." The Hoosiers had already advanced to the championship game, and he wanted an all-Big Ten final, so that was kind of neat of him. We defeated the Beavers by eight to set up our first of three games that season against Indiana.

## A FIRST FIRST

The Hoosiers didn't put up too much of a struggle for the Far West Classic Championship, and we won, 74–57, protecting our No. 4 ranking. It's always good to beat Indiana, but what made it even more wonderful was that by the time we got back to the hotel, the three teams that were ahead of us in the AP and UPI polls had all lost. So Coach said, "Fellas, you may wake tomorrow morning as the No. 1 team in the country."

Sure enough, we did. Michigan State was the top-ranked team for the first time ever, and it was an incredible feeling. The headline in MSU's student newspaper, *The State News*, screamed NO. 1! SPARTANS ARE PERCHED ATOP THE COLLEGIATE BASKETBALL WORLD.

## THERE'S SOMETHING ABOUT MSU, BIG GAMES, AND SNOWSTORMS

The championship game was on December 30, and we were really looking forward to getting back home and celebrating the new year as the new No. 1 team. We also couldn't wait to get a couple of days off before we had to start practicing for the Big Ten opener. Wouldn't you know it? A big snowstorm hit the Pacific Northwest. We took off from Portland and made it to Seattle, but our flight to Detroit made it only as far as Denver, where we stayed for a day.

On New Year's Day we could only get as far as Minneapolis, and we spent the night there. We finally got back to Michigan on January 2, two days before we were supposed to host Wisconsin. We had no chance to revel in being No. 1, because after traveling for three days we had to go right back to practice.

# STARTING OFF ON THE WRONG FOOT

We opened the Big Ten season with an 84–55 win over Wisconsin, but I had one of the worst games of my career. I scored two points—my lowest output since my first game as a freshman when I went scoreless. I was totally ineffective, but Earvin played great and had his second consecutive triple-double, and the third of his career.

Two days later, Minnesota came in with Kevin McHale, Trent Tucker, and Leo Rautins. The Gophers had us down by seven at halftime, and scored the first six points of the second half to boost their lead to 13. Then they started mocking us, saying, "This is the No. 1 team in the country?" They were laughing and just having a good old yuk-yuk time, but that just spurred us on.

It was one of the few times all year when Coach Heathcote decided we weren't going to play our renowned 2-3 matchup zone defense, and put us in a man-to-man. We got ourselves back into the game, took the lead and won, 69–62, but we were playing really differently than we had prior to being ranked No. 1. You could easily sense that we weren't balancing on the perch atop the collegiate basketball world very well. We were trying to hold onto No. 1 as if we already had the title in our hands.

I think the coaches coached differently and we played differently. Something just wasn't right, and things weren't flowing naturally. Everybody was uptight, and hard as this is to believe, Coach was even more vociferous and less patient with mistakes than he had been. And for some reason we were making more mistakes than we normally made. But we were 2-0 in the Big Ten and 9-1 overall and still ranked No. 1 heading into Illinois.

# THE TOAST OF CHAMPAIGN

To this day, the good people in Champaign, Illinois, still talk about our game against the Fighting Illini on January 11, 1979, because they were No. 4, 14-0, and they knocked off the No. 1 team that had Magic Johnson on it. So it's still a big deal in those parts.

What they don't talk about, and probably choose not to remember, is the Illini won only four more games the rest of the season and didn't even get to 20 wins. At least we made their decade and provided them with a lasting a memory.

We kiddingly blamed the loss at North Carolina earlier in the season on Jay Vincent, telling him, "Jay, you blew that game against the Tar Heels when you missed that little bunny from the front of the rim." Well, I got the blame for the Illinois loss because the score was tied and I was guarding Eddie Johnson. With about five seconds left, he got the ball and made a move along the baseline. In my effort to cut him off from the basket, I slipped and lost my footing. When I went down, he shot the jumper at the buzzer for the 57–55 win. So that one was my fault.

# THIS CAN'T BE HAPPENING

We didn't play a good game at Purdue two days later, but we were still tied with the Boilermakers with less than 10 seconds to go. Just like Illinois, they had the ball with time running out. We knocked it loose, and Arnette Hallman, who was a non-shooter and had just one previous basket, grabbed it, turned, and fired from 17 feet. He hit nothing but the bottom of the net as the buzzer sounded. We lost back-to-back games in identical fashion.

# FAVORED BY 20?

In my mind, we hadn't played a good game since leaving Oregon. We certainly weren't playing the way we were capable of playing. We dropped to sixth in the nation before hosting the Indiana Hoosiers, who we had beaten by 17 in the Far West Classic. On the day of the game, Ron Charles and I were in my car and pulling up to the MSU Student Union for our pregame meal when we heard on the radio that we were installed as a 20-point favorite. Bobo and I looked at each other real strangely because we knew we weren't playing well enough at that time to beat anybody by 20 points, let alone a Bobby Knight-coached Indiana team. We kind of laughed about it, but maybe got a subconscious boost. As it turned out, we won by 24, proving that someone knew what he was talking about after all. I think it was just a matter of being back in the familiar surroundings of Jenison Field House where we usually played well. Either way, it was a good bounce-back game for us.

## KEYS TO THE SEASON

We needed overtime to defeat Iowa two days later. We never could stop Hawkeye guard Ronnie Lester, and he had another good game against us. But Mike Brkovich hit two free throws to tie the game up with three seconds to go in regulation.

When I look back at things that needed to happen, and had they not happened, we might not be talking about winning a national championship, Brkovich hitting those two free throws is one of them. We went on to win by 11, but those foul shots were one of the keys to the season. We had the right guy at the line.

## THIS REALLY CAN'T BE HAPPENING

We started to play better, moved back up to No. 4, were 4-2 in the conference, and thought that we still had plenty of time to make things right. More importantly, as we prepared to take on the Wolverines in Ann Arbor, we seemed to be getting back to being the type of team we were before our No. 1 ranking. This was a knockdown, drag-out game, and neither team could get much done. We were again tied with less than 10 seconds to go and they had the basketball. Right at the horn, Keith Smith tried to drive, and they called Earvin for a foul. Smith didn't even go up for a shot, and it seemed crazy the officials would make that call with the game tied, but they did.

It was a one-and-one situation and time had expired, so there was nobody guarding the lane. If Smith made it they would win; if he missed we would go into overtime. Well, he made it of course, and we got beat 49–48. So that loss was Earvin's fault, because he got called for the foul.

# THE SPARTANS HIT BOTTOM

The bottom fell out at Northwestern. The Wildcats hadn't won a game in the conference and hadn't done much of anything all season. Rich Falk, a former great Northwestern player and current Big Ten associate commissioner for officiating programs, was the Wildcat head coach. His team played a perfect game that day and just killed us. We were absolutely listless and had nothing that day. With pro scouts looking on, I scored four big points and played just horribly. Considering how we performed, maybe we should get credit for keeping the blowout to a mere 18 points.

For the first time, I think we let what happened in the preceding game carry over. We had not only lost two days earlier at the buzzer, but we had lost to Michigan. A day-and-a-half of travel in between wasn't enough time for the necessary cleansing. We probably would have lost to anybody that day, but to the Wildcats' credit, they played like the No. 4 team in the nation.

# STATE'S DIRE STRAITS

With four losses in six games, we were 4-4 in the conference, putting us in sixth place and four games behind 8-0 Ohio State. What was so crazy was we'd be ranked no lower than 10th while teams ahead of us in the league standings weren't ranked at all.

What that said was: we were underachieving like crazy. With half the season pretty much gone, 10 games remained in the conference, and Ohio State remained undefeated. There were no odds you could have given anybody that we'd win the Big Ten championship, let alone the national title.

How were we going to overcome that?

# 7

# TAKING THE BACK ROAD TO THE FINAL FOUR

## THE MEETING

One of the critical elements of the 1979 championship run was a team meeting that convened after we dropped to 4-4 in the Big Ten. It's the meeting that everyone still talks about, usually with a less than fair or honest account of what happened. In the urban-myth version, Earvin, some of the other players, and me tell Coach Heathcote in no uncertain terms to back off—his way wasn't working and we were going to start doing things our way. He does, we do, and the result is a national championship, or so the fable goes. Instead of a walkout like the one that occurred four years earlier, we allegedly staged a coup d'état.

Yeah, right. What a bunch of bull.

We got back from Northwestern on Saturday night, took Sunday off and met on Monday. For whatever reason, everybody seems to have a different interpretation of this meeting, which was called by Coach Heathcote. I remember it very, very well.

We were all wedged into the cramped coaches' lounge in Jenison Field House, sprawled out on a sofa, chairs, and the floor. Coach got it started by saying, "Let's talk about our situation, because we're truly at a crossroads. If we're going to salvage this season, we have to re-commit ourselves right here and now. First of all, is there anybody in this room who thinks we cannot do it?"

Of course, no one said he didn't believe we could do it.

Then Coach went around to each guy, and if they had something to say, he wanted to hear it. I was never shy about expressing what was on my mind to Coach Heathcote, so I got up and said, "Coach, I for one think you are on us way too much. We're not able to play comfortably out there. We're too worried about making mistakes, and when a guy does make a mistake the first thing he does is look over his shoulder to the bench. And then there's all the screaming and yelling. I can't play comfortably and I'm a senior. I have got to be able to go out there and just play and not worry about making mistakes."

In recent games Coach had been getting on my case about shooting from outside. I think he had bought into the concept of letting Earvin create everything for us and relying mostly on getting lay-ups. I reminded him that I could shoot the ball, and I could put it on the floor. If I missed or made a mistake, it wasn't intentional and I'd make up for it, but I had to know that it wouldn't be the end of the world.

Earvin got up and talked about the need to push the ball, to run, open things up, and just go. Jay Vincent got up and said, "I just don't know what to do. Everything I do seems to be wrong. You're constantly yelling at me, and it's no fun anymore."

Then Ron "Bobo" Charles pretty much echoed the same thing. However, when Bobo spoke up, Coach was kind of caught off guard. He said, "Ron, I'm not shocked by Gregory, Earvin, or Jay, but I can't believe you have any objections. We always thought you were like a rubber ball that we could throw against the wall and it would bounce right back. You've never been like this." So the rest of the year we called him Rubber Ball.

Then Coach called each remaining guy out by name—Mike Brkovich, Terry Donnelly, and on around the room. One by one they said, "No gripe," "No gripe," "No gripe." I heard "no gripe" so many times I finally stood up and said, "No, they do have a gripe. I'm not trying to speak for anyone, and maybe they're not as comfortable talking to you about this, but they feel the exact same way because we have talked about it amongst ourselves."

I wasn't going to stand there and let that go unchallenged, and I almost felt let down. Coach went to the trouble of opening the door for communication, and they weren't even using it. I could understand it with guys like Gerald Gilkie and Jaimie Huffman—role players whose apprehension was understandable—but what was Terry Donnelly fearful of? What was Mike Brkovich afraid of? They were playing and would continue to play.

Then Mike Longaker got up and talked about the fact that there was way too much talent in the room for us to be struggling the way we were on the floor, and it would really be a crime if it continued. That's what resonated with Coach. That's what he wanted to hear. Then Mike called out Earvin, Jay, and me and asked, who else in the country has this much talent? He made sense in that regard.

I remember reading Earvin's book about how he was the only one who stood up and talked because everybody else clammed up. When I read that, I thought Earvin must have forgotten, because I was the very first one to speak.

At the end of the day, Coach said he would let up and not be as boisterous and vociferous, and would give us more room and flexibility out there. We players promised each other that we would lay everything on the line for the rest of the season and have no excuses. We didn't say we were playing for the NIT, we didn't say we were playing for the NCAA Tournament. We just said we'll play as hard as we possibly can and see where that takes us.

So much for a bloody coup. You weren't taking over Jud Heathcote's team—no way on God's green earth. It was a meeting of the minds, and it came down to a promise from us to play as hard as we could, do our best to concentrate, and cut down on our mistakes. And it was a promise from Coach to ease up on us, let us free flow, let us run, let us make mistakes, let us atone for our mistakes, and most of all just let us have fun, because trust me, it was no fun by then.

# A SECOND MEETING

Later that day at practice, Coach Heathcote shook up the starting lineup. He put Gerald Busby, a very talented freshman guard from Buchanan, Michigan, in Terry Donnelly's spot. He also moved Mike Brkovich ahead of Ron Charles, who had started every game up to that point. We had arguably our best practice of the year, so the meeting turned out to be very good for us.

The next day, however, Gerald Busby withdrew from classes and left school. He was going to get his first career start in two days against Ohio State, but he left, prompting another team meeting. Coach said Gerald quit and went home. Then he asked if he could get Gerald to change his mind, would the players be willing to accept him back? If so, then Coach and his close associate, Silas Taylor, would go to Buchanan. We all liked Busby a lot and thought he could help us. Our overwhelming vote was, "Yes, we want him back." After practice they went to see him, but he didn't want to return. That's how Terry Donnelly got back into the starting lineup.

There were reports that Gerald was homesick, and that he didn't like being at Michigan State because it was too big and overwhelming and he couldn't adjust to the pressure of playing at the Big Ten level. Would we have gone on to win the national championship with Gerald Busby in the starting lineup? We'll never know.

# PUTTING THE AGREEMENT TO THE TEST

Ohio State came into Jenison Field House with a Big Ten record of 8-0, and ranked 13th in the nation. The Buckeyes were beating up everybody. They had Herb Williams, who was a terrific center; Kelvin Ransey, an All-America-caliber guard; and Jim Smith who went on to join Williams and Ransey in the NBA. They came in with a lot of confidence, and figured if they won, they'd put us out of our misery as far as the Big Ten championship was concerned at the halfway point of the league season.

Coach Heathcote promised to lighten up on us, and I thought, "OK, I'm going to test this theory right away." I took a jump shot the first three times I touched the ball. Fortunately, all three went in, so he wouldn't have had anything to complain about anyway.

# WHAT ELSE COULD GO WRONG?

It was late in the first half against Ohio State when Earvin suffered the famous ankle sprain that everyone still talks about. It was pretty severe, and you could see that he was truly hobbled. He wasn't the kind of guy who would over-dramatize a minor injury. We had seen him go down in practice, and he always popped back up. When he didn't get up right away, we were alarmed. As we went past the training room on our way to the locker room at halftime, we could see him getting treatment. Clint Thompson, our trainer, didn't look too optimistic.

When you go into a game knowing you're going to be without a key player, you can deal with it and prepare accordingly. When it happens during the course of game there's no time to prepare or adjust, and it can be devastating. You play with one eye on the game and the other eye toward the training room to see if he's going to return. In this case, we knew we wouldn't be able to beat Ohio State without Earvin.

We started the second half without him, and Jay Vincent, Terry Donnelly, Mike Brkovich, Ron Charles, and I were doing our best to hold things together, but the Buckeyes were undefeated and playing really well.

# ANOTHER URBAN MYTH DEBUNKED

I picked up my fourth foul early in the second half, and Earvin was still in the training room. I was on the bench, and things were looking bleak. We couldn't win without Earvin, but we'd get blown out without both of us.

With about 14 minutes to go, Coach had to make a decision between putting me back in, or continuing to lose control of the game. He decided to put me in. I went to the scorer's table and took a seat on the floor, when all of the sudden I heard a loud roar emanating from the corner of the arena where we entered after leaving the locker room. Those fans were the first to see what was going on, and the din gradually

Everybody points to our home game against Ohio State as the high-water mark of the 1978-79 season because if we didn't pull out a victory against the Buckeyes after Earvin injured his ankle, we very likely wouldn't make it into the NCAA Tournament. The long-forgotten pair of free throws Mike Brkovich made to force overtime against Iowa three games earlier, however, were just as important. They allowed us to avoid losing for the fifth time in the six previous games. *Photo courtesy of Michigan State University*

made its way completely around Jenison. The noise was so intense I thought it was going to tear the roof off.

Coach loves to tell the story that I thought the ovation was for me because I was about to re-enter the game and save the day. It sounds good, and gets him a big laugh every time he tells it, but it's pure fiction. I'm not that vain, and I'm not that crazy. I knew exactly what was going on, and that Earvin was emerging similar to the way Willis Reed limped out for the opening tip when his New York Knicks were playing the Los Angeles Lakers in Game 7 of the NBA Finals back in 1970. I watched that game as a 12-year-old and remember it well, and we were experiencing it for ourselves in Jenison Field House.

We both checked back into the game and sort of restored order, but it was still nip-and-tuck. Earvin was able to make some moves, but he was limping noticeably and didn't have his usual speed. Nevertheless, he had control of the game. He continued to be our primary ball-handler, and Ohio State still couldn't take the ball away from him. Maybe he couldn't blow by anybody, but he's a great leader, and having him on the floor helped restore the calm and confidence necessary to win.

With about 30 seconds to go and MSU leading by four, Ohio State guard Todd Penn took a shot from the top of the key. As the ball was going through the net, an official called a foul on Earvin, who was boxing out underneath. It was a crazy call and the only one we had like that all year, but Buckeye forward Jim Ellinghausen got a one-and-one, and the Buckeyes tied the score with a four-point play. Coach went ballistic. To have a call like that in such a big game was unheard of, but it stood and we went to overtime.

# A SEASON TURNS AROUND IN FIVE MINUTES

Anytime you're at home and you go into overtime, you feel like you've got the edge. We beat Iowa at home in overtime three games earlier, so we felt like we could get it done again. The only issue was foul trouble. I managed to survive with four fouls during the last 13 minutes of regulation, but now I had to go another five. Maintaining our discipline and composure, we won, 84–79, and felt we just passed a major test of our character and maybe got some momentum back. The good news was that if the Buckeyes were to lose their next game to a good Michigan team in Ann Arbor, and we were to win our rematch with Northwestern, we'd be right back in the title hunt.

Thankfully, the Wolverines beat Ohio State, and even though Earvin didn't play in the first half, we beat the Wildcats 61–50. Earvin went in with about five minutes to go, because we went into our 75 Offense and Coach wanted our best ball-handler in the game to help salt away the win. Coach apologized to Earvin afterward, because playing those final minutes hurt his per-game averages.

Just like that, we went from four games out to two games out, and felt like we were OK because the Big Ten was tough, and Ohio State wasn't going to win eight in a row. Plus, we had another crack at the Buckeyes. The pressure of knowing we had to win each of our eight remaining conference games tempered our newfound outlook. Thinking about it in those terms might have been too daunting, however, and as clichéd as it sounds, we took them one game at time and focused only on the one we were playing next.

# SOMEHOW, IT MADE SENSE TO PLAY THREE GAMES IN FOUR DAYS

After we beat Northwestern, we were scheduled to play unranked Kansas the very next day, which was Sunday, February 4, 1979. It was unusual to play a nonconference game that time of year, and it was our third game in four days, but we were looking forward to it. Like us, the Jayhawks made it to the Elite Eight the previous year and they had Paul Mokeski and Darnell Valentine, who had celebrated his birthday the day before. We felt like it was a good opportunity to face a quality team that would challenge us without the pressure of the conference race on our backs. It also was nationally televised. Nowadays it's ho-hum, but back then it was a big deal.

Al McGuire and Dick Enberg broadcast the game for NBC and we played very, very well. Earvin was back in the lineup and moving well on that ankle, and we ran our break to perfection. We scored almost at will, and played good defense while beating them 85–61. I remember watching a replay of the game and Al McGuire wondered out loud how in the world a team like ours could have five losses. We were six points away from being a one-loss team, and if we had been able to overcome those six points we wouldn't have lost by 18 at Northwestern. One way to look at it is we were that close to being undefeated. Another way is, we were still on the brink of elimination.

Regardless, we just came out of a three-game stretch that put us back on solid footing heading into three very tough road games in a row at Iowa, Ohio State, and Indiana.

# EXORCISING DEMONS

Ronnie Lester was having another magnificent game for the Iowa Hawkeyes, their crowd was into it, and we couldn't pull away on their floor. We hung in there and walked away with a three-point win. The last two points came right at the buzzer. As they were pressing, we had the ball out of bounds, I went long, Earvin hit me with a pass, and I dunked it. More importantly, we won a close game. That helped exorcise some demons we were harboring, because aside from the three-point win against Cal State-Fullerton, we had lost all of the other close games.

Our next stop was Columbus, Ohio. The Buckeyes had the revenge factor in their favor, but we won the game by 16 points, which was surprising. What that game did for me individually is make me 8-0 in my career against Ohio State. In an interview after the game, Earvin said, "We're not going to lose any more games." He was only a sophomore, but when he made that statement he spoke for all of us.

# TURNING THE TRIPLE PLAY IN BLOOMINGTON

The last challenge confronting us on the road swing was finding a way to beat Indiana for the third time in the same season. Prior to the 1978-79 season, MSU had only beaten the Hoosiers three times in the previous 15 games dating back to '71. We built a pretty nice lead against IU. I remember going backdoor against Ray Tolbert, and Earvin threw me a lob that was a mile high and headed over the backboard. I usually would go up off two feet to catch his lobs, but I didn't have time to do that because the ball was a foot-and-a-half above the rim, and it had a lot of speed on it. I went off on one foot and then brought the ball from out of bounds with one hand, slamming it through, all in one motion. It was an incredible dunk.

Bobby Knight hated it when his players got beat backdoor. He took Ray Tolbert out and cussed at him real good. We beat Indiana for the third time in a row, and I don't know how many times before that, or since, Bobby Knight lost to the same team three times in the same season.

# FULFILLING A PROPHESY

When that road trip started, I needed 39 points to tie Terry Furlow's MSU all-time scoring record. We figured I would get the bulk of them against Iowa and the rest at Ohio State. I really wanted to break the record in Jenison, but certainly wasn't going to hold back so I could do it at home.

As it turned out, I had 13 against Iowa and 11 at Ohio State. Going into Indiana, I needed 16 to break the record. With the game well in hand I took my 10 points and went into a holding pattern. I didn't attempt a shot in the last four or five minutes, and even passed up an uncontested lay-up. We were in our 75 Offense, and it was my option. Bobo Charles was laughing like mad and said, "If you were trying to break the record at home you would have certainly shot it." And he was absolutely right. I would have. We swept the road trip with me averaging 11 points a game and five points shy of the mark.

After the game, Coach Heathcote said, "We've got three games coming up at home, and Gregory should break the record in the third one."

# A PERFECT STORM BUILDING FOR MICHIGAN

A whole lot of factors were converging for the next home game against Michigan. Despite Coach's comical prediction, there was no doubt I was going to break Terry Furlow's scoring record in that game. As a team, we wanted to avenge the loss on a bad call in Ann Arbor a month earlier, and I wanted to get my first win against the Wolverines in Jenison Field House, which would also be Coach's first home win against them. I was 1-6 versus Michigan, and there were a lot of heated and frosty emotions swirling in the wind.

The Wolverines never had a chance.

I allowed myself to get sky high again for this game because I wanted to feel the euphoria of the win that I knew we were going to get. Coach asked me ahead of time if I would be okay with him not stopping the game to acknowledge the record, because if we were in a flow or on a run, he didn't want to kill it. I played in the game against

Wisconsin when Terry Furlow set the record. They stopped the game, they made a big deal of it, and he threw the ball into the crowd to his girlfriend and mom. I would have liked to have had that as well, but I understood where Coach was coming from—let's keep this thing rolling and not get sidetracked.

The halftime score was 44–14. I was really hoping Coach would let us score 120 on them because to me, a routine victory wasn't going to mitigate all the damage they had done to us during my career. But Coach called off the wolves with five minutes or so left, and we won it 80–57. I scored 20 points and had MSU's all-time scoring record two games ahead of Coach Heathcote's schedule.

## REACHING OUR P-O-T-E-N-T-I-A-L

The next two games were also against teams that had beaten us earlier in the season—Purdue and Illinois. Obviously, revenge was the theme that week. The Boilermakers gave us another tough game, but I had 29 points in the six-point win. I remember picking the ball up off the floor right underneath the basket, going straight up from a standstill, and dunking on Joe Barry Carroll, Purdue's 7-foot-1 All-America center.

We were rolling with eight straight wins, including seven in the conference, since the Northwestern loss, and feeling like we were reaching our potential. That was the team's theme from the start. The Jimmy Castor Bunch had this song called "Potential," and that's where we got it from. We would spell it out in unison: P-O-T-E-N-T-I-A-L. We used to always say if we just played to our potential, it wouldn't matter what the other team did, because we'd win. When we were losing, we were not playing to our potential. Now we were.

## A CURTAIN CALL

My final game at Jenison was against Illinois, and a win would get us back into first place. How good was that, considering we had been four games back with 10 games to go? I was the only senior, and my parents were there, along with my girlfriend and future wife, Donna, and my brother Raymond. Before the game they gave me the ball I broke the scoring record with, and I was able to salute the crowd.

Jack Ebling, the former long-time MSU beat writer and columnist for *The Lansing State Journal*, likes to tell a story about what happened at the very start of that game. As I won the opening tip, the official who threw the ball up had his glasses knocked off. Everybody was streaking to our end of the floor—Michigan State on offense, Illinois on defense—and out of the side of my eye I happened to see the ref scrambling around for his glasses, which he couldn't see. So I backtracked, picked up the glasses, and placed them in his hand before rejoining the action.

It was no big deal to me, but it got played up in the newspaper the next day. I guess it said something about me to some people. I suppose they thought it was a classy move, but I just saw a man struggling to find his vision and I lent a hand. It was probably a matter of me being the only one to see what happened. But hey, I didn't foul out and went out in style with 24 points and nine rebounds. It turned out to be Earvin's last home game as well, and he bowed out with a triple-double—21 points, 11 rebounds, and 11 assists.

We won by 14, but it wasn't that close, and we were back in first place. Everything was falling into place.

# A SENSE OF ACCOMPLISHMENT

I got a big surprise at breakfast on the morning of our second-to-last regular season game at Minnesota. I had been named All-America along with Earvin. This was tremendous for me, because I'm the guy who always got short-changed when it came to that kind of stuff.

Keep in mind that I averaged 22 points and nearly 11 rebounds per game as a sophomore. That's a 20-10 double-double. Stan Washington, with 21 points and 11 rebounds per game in 1964-65, is the only other Spartan to do that. Minnesota's Kris Humphries was a first-team All-Big Ten selection when he averaged 21.7 points and 10.1 rebounds 2004, but all I rated was second team. I was second team my junior year as well, despite averaging 18 points and nine rebounds while helping MSU win its first Big Ten championship in 11 years. I was never once the Big Ten Player of the Week in four years.

So when the All-America notification came, it was a shock. And what did Coach Heathcote say about that? "Well, tonight you have to go out and play like one." Never mind I had been playing like one since the Northwestern loss.

We beat the Gophers 76–63, with Earvin scoring 25 points, me with 23, and Jay Vincent chipping in 21. Together, we scored all but seven of our points.

That game was the only time I ever had a dunk blocked and sent back at me. I was one-on-one against Kevin McHale. He saw me and I saw him, and I took the ball back a little bit farther than usual because I really wanted to punish the rim and him. By trying to be overemphatic, it gave him an opportunity to get his timing together and force in the right place. We met right at the summit, and it was like an arm-wrestling match. I couldn't turn it over, and he rejected it without fouling, but it didn't matter because we won the game. Iowa, the team we were tied with, lost to Michigan in Iowa City, putting us in sole possession of the conference lead. How about those Wolverines doing us two favors by beating the Buckeyes when they were three games ahead of us in February, and downing the Hawkeyes in the second-to-last conference game of the season. We desperately needed both of those things to happen.

# DEMON MAKES A COMEBACK

All we had to do is win at Wisconsin, and we'd be outright Big Ten champs for the second straight year. Well, long story short, we got to Wisconsin and it was well known that if the Badgers lost, head coach Bill Cofield would probably be fired.

The score was 81–79 their favor, and Earvin went to the foul line with three seconds to go. Like Mike Brkovich in the game against Iowa, he knocked down both free throws to tie the game. As they got ready to inbound, we pressured the ball to keep it in front of us so they couldn't throw long. Instead of attempting a long throw, they inbounded the ball from underneath our basket to Wes Matthews who was standing in front of our bench. He took a couple of dribbles, and let the ball go from well beyond halfcourt. It was about a 60-foot shot. It's amazing how time can stand still. As I watched the ball sail through the air, I could seemingly read the name and logo on it, and the doggone thing never left its line. From where I was standing, it looked like it was going to be a direct hit, and all the while scary thoughts are going through my mind, "Is this going to be another Illinois, another Purdue, another Michigan. Is this déjà vu?"

I instantly got my answer. Yes!

The ball hit the backboard and banked in, we lost by two points and their crowd went crazy. We ended up in a three-way tie for first place. It was a letdown because we had won 10 straight games and wanted to close things off the way we said we would. The epitaph on our regular season was five losses at or after the buzzer, and one blowout.

# ANOTHER KELSER MILESTONE

With 10 boards against Wisconsin, I passed Johnny Green to become MSU's all-time leading rebounder, which I still am to this day with 1,092. Coach Heathcote congratulated me but also reminded me that the milestone came in a loss. He could have saved his breath. I was well aware of that fact and found no joy in the feat because we lost the game. It was a great day for the Badgers but not for us after going nearly five weeks without tasting defeat. But Earvin said something afterward that helped me immensely. "Their season is over, let them celebrate. We've still got the tournament in front of us."

# A MASTER OF PSYCHOLOGY

Coach's promise to us in that meeting following the humiliation at Northwestern lasted about two games, and then he was back to his old self, getting on us and challenging guys to not make stupid mistakes. But we were playing much better and not looking over to the sideline nearly as much.

Coach was such a master of psychology he would let you think you were in control and getting it done your way, when in actuality you were doing it his way. If letting you think you were somehow in control made you play better, then he went with it. Coach knows only one way, and he didn't change back in January. If he were to come out of retirement right now, he'd still coach the way he always did. Maybe it was just the winning, because we truly became a galvanized unit when our backs were up against it. Maybe the yelling sounded the same; it just didn't feel the same.

# OUT OF THE GAUNTLET

We finished tied for the championship with Iowa and Purdue, but we knew we were in the NCAA Tournament even before the newly expanded 40-team field was selected because two Big Ten teams had gone every year since '75. We swept the Hawkeyes and split with the Boilermakers so we weren't worried.

As it turned out, the NCAA selected MSU and Iowa, and Purdue ended up going to the NIT. It shows how tough it was to get into the NCAA Tournament when one of the Big Ten tri-champs doesn't get in. Indiana also went to the NIT and beat the Boilers for the championship, so that shows you how strong the Big Ten was in '79.

We felt good going into the tournament because of our success against nonconference teams. We were out of the Big Ten gauntlet, and the teams we were going to face didn't know us and weren't going to have a lot of time to prepare for a 6-foot-9 point guard, our overall size, and athletic ability.

# DEALING WITH LAMAR'S INSOLENCE

When the parings came out, we were the No. 2 seed in the Mideast Region, and Notre Dame was No. 1. That was kind of cool because we figured we'd finally get a chance to meet the Irish. We were among the 24 teams that got a first-round bye and would play the winner of the game between No. 7 Detroit and No. 10 Lamar in Murfreesboro, Tennessee. We spent the whole week practicing for Detroit with Terry Duerod and Earl Cureton because that's who we thought was going to win.

We didn't spend one minute thinking about Lamar. We watched that game on Friday night, and Lamar, with a pair of forwards named B.B. Davis and Clarence Kea and coached by Billy Tubbs, was handling

U of D. We were stunned when Lamar won the game. Then we watched Davis and Kea's interview after the game. I think it was Kea who said, "Well, we've taken care of Detroit, and we'll take care of Michigan State on Sunday, and that will be it for the State of Michigan." You look for motivation wherever you can grab it, and that's what we took to practice with us that Saturday as we began to prepare for the fearless Cardinals.

The Lamar players were watching us warm up before the game and cracking jokes about Coach Heathcote's comb-forward haircut. All that did was get us more and more stoked to destroy these guys. The closest that game ever was, was at the opening tip, because we ran out on them early. Davis and Kea, with 10 and 11 points, respectively, weren't factors. I had 31 points and 14 rebounds, Earvin had 13 points, 17 rebounds, and 10 assists, and we dispatched them easily, 95–64. It could have been a whole lot worse.

## A TALE OF TWO FEET

The only negative about the Lamar game was that Jay Vincent, who was killing them and had 11 points in the first half, sustained a stress fracture in his foot. That was also the game when Coach put our bench in with about five minutes to go, and Jaimie Huffman lost his shoe. He spent about a minute of playing time he rarely got—and precious NCAA Tournament seconds—getting his shoe back on as play went up and down the court without him. That's when Al McGuire made the statement that Jaimie will forever be remembered as "Shoes" Huffman. When we got back to East Lansing, he went from obscurity to being a celebrity, but we continued to call Jaimie by his given nickname, "Brickmeister."

## TIT FOR TAT AND NO EXCUSES

Our Mideast Regional semifinal was against LSU in Indianapolis. They were a very good basketball team, but their first-team All-Southeastern Conference guard and leading scorer, DeWayne "The Astronaut" Scales, was suspended for talking to an agent. We felt, hey, we don't have Jay—whoopee, it's even. Ron Charles had a super game with 18 points and 14 rebounds and everybody else played well. We held them to 19 points in the first half and came out of it with an uneventful 87–71 victory.

# A BIT O' FIGHTIN' IRISH MALARKY

It seemed like Notre Dame was playing head games.

They truly let us know we were the No. 2–seeded team in that region because they had the option of what uniform to wear, and they chose their home colors which meant we had to wear all green. We wore our white home uniforms in each of the previous two games because we were the higher seed. We wore our whites in the national championship game, even though Indiana State was a No. 1 seed and the No. 1–ranked team in the country. Then, when the Irish came out wearing lime-green uniforms, we thought we could have worn our whites after all. But it was no problem for us, because we looked good winning in green, too.

At the press conference the day before the game, the Irish talked about having to wear football helmets and shoulder pads because MSU is a physical team and they were prepared to be knocked around. We thought that was strange because we never fashioned ourselves as being very physical. We came out of the physical Big Ten and were a good defensive team, but other than Jay Vincent, we didn't have anybody who could out-muscle anyone—and Jay was hurt. We certainly didn't have bulk like Notre Dame had with Bill Laimbeer and Bruce Flowers, but they put the physical tag on us. We dismissed it as a psychological ploy, or maybe them trying to plant seeds ahead of time with the officials.

It's not like they had to resort to such tactics. They were a very dominant team and had been to the previous Final Four. Laimbeer, Orlando Woolridge, Kelly Tripucka, and Bill Hanzlik all went on to have long NBA careers; and Flowers and Tracy Jackson also made it to the NBA.

# COACH HEATHCOTE RESPONDS

Coach Heathcote never overlooked any detail, and even though it was late in the season, he put in two new plays for the Irish. It speaks directly to the coaching prowess of Jud Heathcote that he realized Notre

Dame never put anybody back in a defensive position on the opening tip, and he immediately devised a way to exploit it.

I had only lost two jump balls during my entire career, but I always used to tap backwards, gain possession of the ball, walk it up the floor and get into our halfcourt set.

Coach came to me at practice and said, "Orlando Wooldridge is 6-foot-9 and a high-jumping kind of guy, but do you think you can outjump him?"

I was 6-foot-7, but I said, "Yeah, why not? I won it against everybody else including guys taller than him."

Then he said, "If they don't put anybody back this time, I want you to tip forward to Earvin, and he will re-direct to Mike Brkovich, who'll be streaking to the basket. We're going to see if we can get a bucket right off the bat." We practiced it quite a bit the day before the game, and I told Mike, "When you get it, don't lay it up. Get good and loose in warmups because you need to make a resounding opening statement by dunking that ball."

We worked on another play for me. I'd flash into the post from the weak side, get the ball in the middle of the lane and shoot my little turnaround jumper. Coach felt I could use my quickness in the paint to get some opportunities. We had never run the play before, and I recall getting frustrated because when we did in practice, the scouting team kept making the play. They knew what was coming and would jump in and intercept the pass, or collapse on me and block my shot from behind. Coach was getting mad at me because I wasn't able to execute the play, and everybody else was laughing at me. I was angry with my teammates because they made me the butt of their joke, and finally I just yelled out, "I can't do it. Run it for somebody else." To which Coach Heathcote replied, "Dammit, get back in there. You're going to run this play." He made me do it until we got it right, even though the scouting team never stopped making the play.

## HOW DO YOU SOLVE A PROBLEM LIKE GREGORY?

Coach Heathcote hates it when I tell this story, but it happened. Jay Vincent and I were roommates at the team hotel in downtown

Indianapolis. Jay's girlfriend and my girlfriend, Donna, were staying with my folks at a hotel about 10 miles away. After we had dinner as a team, we had free time until our 11 p.m. curfew. At about 7:30, we borrowed a car and visited our girlfriends and my family. We had a nice time, and at about 10:15 started making our way back, but we got lost. We were all turned around, it was getting pretty close to 11:00 and here I am, a team captain about to miss bed check the night before our big game against Notre Dame. Jay was incredibly nervous because he was really intimidated by Jud. I was too, but maybe didn't show it as much.

Finally, something hit him like a lightning bolt, and he said, "Why am I worrying? I'm with you." He figured Coach wasn't going to do anything to me, so he's in the clear. We finally got back by 11:15 and thought we sneaked in. When we got up to our room, I called our manager, Darwin Payton, and said, "Dar, did Coach check our room?" And he said, "Yeah, man, and he is angry. You better call him."

I called Coach, I let him know we were back and tried to explain what happened, but he didn't want to hear about it and hung up on me. At breakfast the next morning it was most somber and Coach said, "Guys we've got a big game today, but for some reason we've got two guys who chose to do things their own way last night." He really put us on the spot, and we felt bad because it wasn't something we did intentionally. We just got lost. Then he said, "We're still going to try to keep our attention on what we need to do." I apologized to him and the team and said this was a very poor time for something like this to happen.

# IRWIN "MAGIC" JOHNSON?

As luck would have it, I missed my first six shots against Notre Dame, and things just continued to not go well. However, we did get that opening tip and Brkovich did dunk it. Then Terry Donnelly stole the ensuing inbounds pass, and I think we knocked the Irish off balance from the very beginning.

Bill Hanzlik drew a charge from Earvin early in the game, and as he got up from the floor—and you could hear it on the television replay—he said, "Not today, Irwin." There was a lot of talk going back and forth. We had three really good officials in that game and about midway through the first half, and the courtside microphone picked this up too, one of the refs telling us, "OK guys, we had a good game going here for awhile. Now it's just a bunch of horseshit, and I need you to clean it up."

What he was saying was cut out the cheap shots, stop the talking, and play basketball. It was hard to do that against a team like Notre Dame, and I'm sure they felt the same way about us. We were standing in each other's way of getting to the Final Four.

## JAY VINCENT'S BRIEF BUT TRIUMPHANT COMEBACK

Even though we had an 11-point halftime lead, we couldn't really put Notre Dame away. At one point in the second half we kind of got bogged down and needed a lift, so Coach summoned Jay off the bench. He was noticeably limping on that broken foot, but shortly after he got in, he caught the ball near the top of the key where he was being guarded by Bill Laimbeer. Now Laimbeer's a smart player, and he knew Jay was less than 100 percent. Probably thinking there was no way Jay was going to go by him, Laimbeer got right up on him; but Jay pump-faked like he was going to shoot the jumper, and Bill went for it. Jay put the ball on the floor, limped around Laimbeer and got a lay-up, and we all got to experience the Willis Reed effect for the second time in 14 games. Reed scored only four points against the Lakers in Game 7 of the 1970 NBA Finals, but his presence and his courage, and the fact he was out there doing what he could, inspired his teammates to win the championship that night. Right after Jay beat Laimbeer, our crowd went crazy. We got a surge of energy and made a run to go up by 18 points.

It was a dunk that got me off the schneid, and then I went on to hit 15 of my next 19 shots, because I ended up making 15 of 25. There was stretch where I had 18 points in six minutes and that was when things opened up for us. We got some dunks, Earvin threw some lobs, we were running and jumping, we were quicker, and I don't think Notre Dame had ever been blitzed like that or outplayed from an athletic standpoint. We did whatever we wanted. We got nine dunks, and we never did that against anybody else. I had six by myself. And, *we were physical.* So maybe they recognized something we hadn't even known about ourselves. We were very good that day and proved we were clearly the better team. I came out with about a minute to go, and Irish coach Digger Phelps was very gracious. He shook my hand and wished me luck in the Final Four. That was a nice touch, because it had to be a very difficult moment for him.

I scored 36 points, but it says I had 34 points in the record book, because they gave Ron Charles one of my tap-ins It was the fourth basket Bobo got that belonged to me during the three years we played together.

Coach came into the locker room after the game and said to me, "You know what, you might have earned yourself a few dollars today."

## FATHER'S DAY IN MARCH

One of the nice things about that win is it came on March 18, which is my dad's birthday. The loss to Kentucky in the regional finals the year before also came on March 18. So I gave him a nice birthday present. It just took an extra year.

## NOT THE TRUE NATIONAL CHAMPIONSHIP GAME

A lot of people feel the Michigan State–Notre Dame showdown was the real national championship game in 1979 because had the Irish advanced to the Final Four in Salt Lake City, they would have been favored to beat the other teams. I'm not of that mind. How could anyone disregard Indiana State, which was undefeated, ranked No. 1, and had Larry Bird?

# 8

# THE FINAL FOUR THAT CHANGED COLLEGE BASKETBALL

## ALWAYS THINKING

During our first practice back in East Lansing after beating Notre Dame to advance to the Final Four, Coach Heathcote openly contemplated leaving early for Salt Lake City. He wanted to cut down on distractions, get us used to the altitude, and keep us reined in as a team. If we were at home, we had freedom of movement and could scatter. It's not that we were going to get in any trouble, but why even take a chance that something unforeseen would happen to us?

Coach was two wins away from his own dream come true, and he was going to do everything to maximize our chances for success. He was on top of anything. Without much more deliberation, Coach had us do just that. We left on Wednesday, whereas Pennsylvania, our national semifinal opponent, and DePaul and Indiana State on the other side of the bracket, didn't get out there until Thursday for practice on Friday.

We had two grueling practices in Salt Lake. I think it was Coach's way of bringing us back down and not letting us get too caught up in ourselves. It didn't feel anything like we thought a Final Four ought to feel. It felt like preseason camp in October. By the time the other three teams joined us in Utah, we sensed we had a clear advantage. They had practiced at their gyms in Philadelphia, Chicago, and Terre Haute, but we were settled in, and our concentration was where it needed to be.

## WHAT TO MAKE OF PENN

Sometimes I get the impression that people think we had an easy path to the national championship game because we played Penn. Based on our 101–67 victory, maybe we did, but it didn't look that way going in. At least we did our best not to let it look that way. The Quakers defeated the same North Carolina team we had lost to earlier in the season. And, they beat Syracuse, who we lost to the year before. We told ourselves we couldn't take those guys lightly. Earvin might have had some dismissive things to say about Penn, but he could get away with it because he was going to play the same way regardless if we were playing Penn, Lansing Community College, or the Detroit Pistons. Nevertheless, we kept trying to find something to motivate us. Usually you can get it by reading the newspapers or watching TV, but all we could come up with was them saying that we wouldn't be dunking on them like we did on Notre Dame. That was it.

## DOMESTIC LIFE AT THE FINAL FOUR

I roomed with Jay Vincent in Salt Lake City, and Earvin roomed with Ron "Bobo" Charles. All of our families came out to support us. My girlfriend, Donna, was there. Earvin and Jay's girlfriends were there, but Ron's girlfriend Penny wasn't. Every night on the phone she used to give him hell for it. Earvin told us about some of the conversations he overheard and we laughed about them in practice. Earvin said that whenever their conversation was coming to an end, Ron would try to get in an "I love you" on the sly. He'd just kind of mumble, "I love you, I love you, I love you." That apparently wasn't good enough for Penny back in East Lansing, and in an effort to just cut the conversation off and hang up, Ron would finally blurt, "*I love you! I love you!*" The conversations invariably didn't begin until late into the night, so Penny would wake up both Earvin and Ron, and Earvin would complain about not getting enough sleep. I always felt Ron figured he needed all of his concentration to play, and Penny could be a little distracting. While I never asked, I felt the separation was by design. Smart man, that Bobo.

## GETTING ON A ROLL

We played in the first game on Saturday and I remember Coach being pretty calm. Traditionally, after Penn scored its first basket its fans would throw rolls of toilet paper out on the floor. They scored and out came the streams of paper. We responded by rolling over the Quakers with a 30–6 burst. You don't typically see runs like that in the Final Four, but we got an unbelievable surge, and Penn went eight and a half minutes without scoring. The Quakers were hurrying their shots and missing layups. Maybe they were nervous. When they finally ended their scoring drought, our fans cheered for them. Penn was a very good team, but we weren't losing to anybody that day. With the score 50–17 at the half, we knew that game was over and we were in the final. We wouldn't have blown a 33-point lead to an NBA team.

I remember what Coach said at halftime very well. He talked about not embarrassing Penn. He acknowledged that we still had to play the second half, but let's not show them up with any unnecessary antics. He also reminded us that we did not want to embarrass ourselves either—play fundamentally sound basketball and keep it classy. We won the first half by 33 points and we won the second half by one, and our reserves enjoyed considerable Final Four playing time.

## CONTEMPLATING
## DEMONS AND SYCAMORES

Late in the Penn game, our fans were chanting: "We want Bird! We Want Bird!"

To which the Indiana State fans replied: "You'll Get Bird! You'll Get Bird!"

After we finished off the Quakers, we sat in the stands with our families and watched the first half of the DePaul–Indiana State game. It was back and forth, and Larry Bird was putting on quite a show. He was unstoppable, but DePaul was a very good team, and Mark Aguirre wasn't too shabby himself. What I remember most about that Blue Demon team was that Ray Meyer, a great coach and a very nice man, almost never substituted. He played his starters the whole game most of the year, and if he did substitute it was with one guy who might get three minutes. He rode his five starters most of the whole way. I thought if we played DePaul on Monday night we'd have the edge because we would run, and we might be able to get them in foul trouble; then what would they do?

From watching Indiana State, I thought our best chance to defeat the Sycamores would be by taking Bird and Carl Nicks away as much as possible and make their other guys beat us. By limiting Purdue center Joe Barry Carroll's effectiveness, we won the second game against the Boilermakers that way.

We left at halftime because sitting there didn't serve any useful purpose. We were so in tune with what we were doing, and believed supremely that if we did what we did best it wouldn't matter which team we played. We got back to the hotel in time to catch the last six minutes of the game, and it was so tight we didn't know the identity of our next opponent until Aguirre's shot to tie the game bounced off the rim in the waning seconds.

We knew Indiana State had just improved to an impressive 33-0. We also knew the Sycamores barely scraped by in their previous two games, beating Arkansas 73–71 in the regional final, and DePaul 76–74 in the national semifinal. Meanwhile, we won our four tournament games by an average of 22 points. Soon we were embracing the idea of going against Larry Bird, who was the national player of the year.

# SUNDAY PRACTICE

We got to the arena for Sunday's practice a little early. Indiana State was still finishing up, so we waited in the hallway. Finally the Sycamores left the floor and as they strutted past us they were chanting and whooping and hollering, and getting all pumped up. The corridor was only so wide, and we could have reached out and touched them. We felt it was all directed toward us, but we just watched dispassion-ately. Like I said, you try to find motivation anywhere you can, and we took that as an affront—real or imagined. It wasn't like it would be today with handshakes and hugs and all of that BS. No way. Larry Bird wasn't looking for cordial conversation and neither were we.

# THE LARRY BIRD SHOW STARRING MAGIC JOHNSON

Each member of our scouting team represented an opposing player. The biggest problem we faced in practice was finding someone on our scouting team who could mimic Bird. We didn't have anybody who was 6-foot-9 and could shoot from way out, or passed as deftly, or did all the things he did for Indiana State. So for the first time ever, Coach Heathcote put Earvin on the scouting team. Earvin was Larry Bird for a day. It made brilliant sense. He was 6-foot-9, could pass with the best, and it didn't matter if he could make shots from way outside. He just had to take them.

Coach decided to stay with our 2-3 matchup zone, but we were going to modify it. If Larry Bird was in your specific area, he was your man. When he got the ball we'd send another defender his way. Essentially, once Larry made his move to the basket, we would have two guys on him, and our other three were responsible for his four teammates.

Earvin loved being Larry Bird, and he put on an incredible show. He was shooting from long distance, and they were going in. Coach was just going nuts because the more we'd get up on Magic Bird, the farther out he would go, and he kept on making them. He was passing to guys, and Rick Kaye and Don Brkovich were scoring on us with impunity. Coach was really getting irritated and said, "If we can't stop E, how in the hell are we going to stop Bird?"

The only starter to enjoy practice that day was Earvin. He enjoyed the freedom to shoot he rarely had when he was Magic.

# MONDAY, MONDAY

It's the craziest thing. From the instant we knew we were going to the Final Four, everything seemed to go so fast that you couldn't take a minute to understand the magnitude of what you were doing and enjoy the once-in-a-lifetime experience. Then when we finally had some down time, it was pure agony. That Monday was the longest day of my life. We went to breakfast and then to the shootaround, which was a lot of fun. Coach was in a good mood, and we shot for quarters. Some of the guys even came out of it a buck or two richer. Once we got back to the hotel, we had seven hours to kill. We read, watched TV, tried to nap—we tried anything to keep from burning nervous energy. But we knew we were on the threshold of something big, and it was difficult to relax.

## BUTTERFLIES AREN'T FREE

The waiting was terrible and nothing flowed like it usually did before a game. It was the most nervous I have ever felt. I had butterflies and was jittery. After we finally made our way to the arena, the butterflies actually got worse. I went through warmups and the lay-up line wondering how long it was going to take to shake this, because I had never felt like that before. I don't know how the other guys felt, but as a captain and a senior, and someone who had to play well for us to be successful, dealing with something new like that was disconcerting, but I didn't let anyone know about it. When the time to toss the ball up finally approached, I started to exterminate some of those butterflies. Getting back into my element must have done it.

I have to be honest. I don't remember anything from Coach's pregame speech, and I was usually pretty good about soaking up that kind of stuff. Maybe it was because of the jitters and being really worried about what was going on inside of me, because I couldn't have played well feeling like that.

I remember reading that Bill Russell would throw up before big games and that was the only way he could play. I wasn't to that point, but something needed to happen to calm me down. Fortunately all it took was for the game to start. I knew I was okay when I beat Alex Gilbert, their center who was a high flyer like me and rarely lost jump balls, on the opening tip. We got the first possession, and everything was all right.

## INDIANA STATE ALSO HAS A FEW TRICKS UP ITS SLEEVE

We were really surprised when Larry Bird came out guarding me. One would have thought they would have put Bird on someone else, like Ron Charles, because Ron would not run him around and sap his energy on the defensive end like I would.

## MAKING MY OWN KIND OF MAGIC

Without prior announcement or consciously changing anything, I became more of a passer that night. It was great because it was something I could do, and it was almost like going back to my sophomore year when I did a lot of the ball-handling. From the time Earvin came on board the following year, he was the hub of our offense for two seasons right up to that final game. For some strange reason, I had the ball in my hands a lot against Indiana State. I was able to drive by Larry, but when I'd get into the lane maybe Gilbert would leave his man and cut me off. The first time I touched the ball I drove inside, drew Gilbert over to me, and dropped it off to Ron Charles. Ron dunked it and I had assist No. 1. I did that a lot that night. The one thing I could do against Larry is beat him with my first step off the dribble, so I was constantly in the lane. He could not deal with my foot speed. I'd get in the lane and drop it off to Earvin, or kick it out to Terry Donnelly.

This is what Earvin normally did, but now I was doing it because we were taking advantage of my ability to challenge Larry. A couple of times I was able to get into the lane and finish myself. I think it really showed the versatility of each and every guy on our team that we could change roles and still get it done.

That night, I became the triple-double threat. The points and rebounds were a given, but nobody expected the assists. I was just taking what was there.

## TAMING THE UNTAMABLE BIRD

We seized control of the game, and it was clear the strategy with our zone was working because Bird was very frustrated. At various times, he had 6-foot-8 Ron Charles, 6-foot-7 Greg Kelser, 6-foot-9 Earvin Johnson, or 6-foot-8 Jay Vincent guarding him with help from

Terry Donnelly or Mike Brkovich. We did a very good job of cutting off his passing lanes and making him score over the top of us. With our long arms he was changing some of his shots by arcing them a little higher to keep them from being blocked or tipped.

To show the intensity of Larry Bird, though, I remember when Indiana State's sixth man, Leroy Staley, came into the game. Jay got an offensive rebound on him and Staley fouled him. You can hear Bird on videotape chastising Staley, "Godammit Leroy, check him out!" That was an all-out challenge. It seemed a little odd at that stage but hey, Bird was the unquestioned leader of that team, and I'm sure he did that all year while the Sycamores were winning 33 straight games.

# ALL'S FAIR IN BASKETBALL, WAR, AND BROADCASTING

Bird hit me in the first half as he came over the middle on a baseline out-of-bounds play under our basket. He got me square in the chest with his shoulder, and I thought he cracked it. He nailed me right in the perfect spot and stood me straight up for a second. When you get hit in the sternum like that, it's very painful to breathe. It settled down enough for me to continue, but I dealt with it the rest of the game.

A few plays later, we were in front of our bench and underneath their basket. Larry got the ball and I was right there on him with Terry Donnelly. He leaned in and hit me again in the chest with his shoulder while trying to clear space to get the shot off. I hit the floor and the official called a charge on Larry. He drilled me too, right on that same spot.

I was somewhat amused while watching a tape of the television broadcast a few weeks later when Billy Packer—then a color commentator for NBC—said I flopped on the play. He said Bird barely hit me. Maybe that's how it looked to him while watching the replay in slow motion, but when it happened I thought I was going to have to be wheeled off the floor on a stretcher.

# THE DREADED "MICROCOSM" EFFECT

We led by nine at halftime, feeling pretty comfortable with where we were and what we were able to get done. The only issue was that Earvin and I each had three fouls. Unlike today when coaches yank you out of the first half when you get your second foul, back then it was three and you come out. We continued to roll in the second half, and just like that, we were up by 16 points. This game was taking on the same complexion as those against Penn and Lamar, where we just stretched it out and never looked back.

Of course, *our* national championship couldn't possibly come in a neatly wrapped package. It had to mirror everything we had been through up to this point. The ultimate game had to fall into that hackneyed "microcosm-of-the-season" category.

Our slide began when I got the ball on the right side of the floor. Larry Bird was covering me and Earvin was posting. I crossed over to my left hand and tried to go left-hand dribble into the lane to maybe finish for myself or drop it off like I had been doing. As I made my move, Larry sort of leaned in, but he didn't square up in front of me. When we made contact, shoulder to shoulder, he went down. The official came over and pointed at me for my fourth foul with 17:22 to go. It was a very questionable call, but I had to go to the bench where I sat for eight excruciating minutes. It felt like an hour because our offense just came to a halt.

They were able to key on Earvin, and Mike Brkovich wasn't having his normal game and couldn't get open. Fortunately, Terry Donnelly had the hot hand and made all five of his shots and five of six free throws, but then they stopped leaving him open. Jay was playing at 30-percent capacity with his foot, and Ron was pretty much staying inside. What we were suddenly missing was someone who could create for himself and his teammates, which was the role I was providing before leaving the game.

We started holding the ball, and our defense changed because while Jay was gutting it out, he wasn't as mobile, and Larry started finding openings and hitting some shots. We were bogged down and turning it over, and slowly but surely our lead started to dwindle—16 points, 14, 12, and then 10. All I could do was sit there and helplessly watch. When it got to eight points it was even tougher, because I was thinking we might be in a dogfight with these guys.

## COULD IT BE DÉJÀ VU?

Then my mind went back to all the close games we lost during the year—one point at North Carolina, two points at Purdue and Illinois, one point at Michigan, two points at Wisconsin. I said to myself, "I don't want this to be close. I don't want to take any chances of it coming down to the last 10 seconds and not having the ball." I didn't want that bad karma to come back, but our lead was down to six points, and the Indiana State fans were into it big time. The Sycamores hadn't lost all year, and I was pretty sure they had fought back from some deficits before and felt they could do it again because they just knocked 10 points off our 16-point lead.

Coach signaled for me to go back in with about nine minutes to go, and it was my job to help re-establish our offensive flow, defend because it's a game again, rebound and not commit another foul. Right away, I went one-on-one against Larry Bird in the lane and scored from 14 feet, but I was playing tentatively on defense. I tried to avoid contact and I wasn't going for blocked shots because I was going to stay on the floor some way, somehow. Once I re-entered the game, our confidence came back and we mellowed out. I'm glad coach took the gamble and got me in there when he did instead of waiting until two minutes remained. It gave me enough time to get back in the flow and get the sweat going again, and we had a little cushion to work with.

## HOW TO MAKE A MAGAZINE COVER

We restored a 10-point lead, and my last assist came with me standing at the top of the key with the ball. Earvin went back door, I got him the ball and he went in and dunked on Indiana State guard Bob Heaton for the pose that is frozen for all time on the cover of *Sports Illustrated*. Earvin also got the low-bridge call and made both free throws for a four-point play that went our way for a change. Our lead was back to 10, and whenever we'd get up by double digits near the five-minute mark, Coach put us into our 75 Offense to work for lay-ups and foul shots. Our spread offense worked well, and a little later when they were really pressuring up, we were able to throw long a couple times. I got a dunk on a run-out when they were pressing Earvin, and he hit me deep. That was the first nail in their coffin.

## PUTTING AN EXCLAMATION POINT ON A SPECIAL K-AREER

Late in the game, when there was no doubt we'd win, Indiana State took a shot and almost simultaneously, Earvin yelled, "Go Greg, go!" I took off. He got the ball out of the basket, stepped out of bounds and threw it over his shoulder. I caught the ball near midcourt and at that point I'm thinking, "How do I want to dunk this?" because I had a vast array of dunks. I thought about doing a 360, I thought about throwing it against the backboard, catching it and slamming it home. The one thing you can't do is miss it. You also have to consider that it's late in the game, you've just played 30-some minutes, and you might not have the legs you had at the beginning. I finally decided to go with something safe so I cuffed it, cradled it, and windmilled it.

That play ended the game for us, symbolically ended my career, and began our reign as national champions. I had 19 points, eight rebounds, and a career-high nine assists in 32 minutes—the same as my jersey number. It was a beautiful thing and the highlight of my career.

## TEARS WERE GOING TO BE SHED

After we won, 75–64, Larry Bird came over and shook our hands and then went to his bench where Mel Daniels, an Indiana State assistant coach, consoled him. Larry had a towel over his face and I'm sure he was shedding a few tears. People often ask me, "What was it like to make Larry Bird cry?" Hey, Larry Bird was a fierce competitor. It was either going to be him or us—somebody was going to be crying that night.

Larry had 19 points and 13 rebounds, but only two assists. That was the big thing. Not only did we make things tough for him as he shot 7-for-21, but we limited his impact on his teammates. We didn't allow him to make them better, and that's why we won the game. They may have been able to survive a poor shooting night from him if he would have gotten 10 assists. However, even though he struggled he was the most difficult cover of anybody we played that year. He was a tougher defensive dilemma than Mike Woodson, who always torched us; than Kelvin Ransey, who always got his numbers against us; than Joe Barry Carroll, who got 27 points and was the high scorer against us that season.

It started on that Sunday when we had to take one of the best players ever to play the game and put him on the scouting team to mimic Larry Bird. Afterward, I knew Larry was going to be a super, super player at the pro level where the game really opens up, he'd be surrounded by better teammates, and opponents would be unable to get away with putting two defenders on him. I wasn't the least bit surprised when he had a great rookie year and became a fantastic NBA player.

## THAT'S SO TYPICAL

While we were celebrating and hugging on the floor, a reporter from one of the local papers pulled me to the side, and I did a quick interview with him while Earvin and Coach Heathcote did an interview with Bryant Gumbel, who was a sports commentator for NBC at the time. I should have stayed with my group so I could have gotten some national face time, but as usual, I was being a nice guy.

## WHAT, NO CHAMPAGNE?

I stepped into the locker just for a moment, exchanged a couple of quick embraces, and then Coach Heathcote took Terry, Earvin, and me to the press conference. We were still in our uniforms and stayed there for what seemed like forever. When we got back to the locker room, everybody was already gone. It was just the three of us and Coach. It was weird. Like I said, everything during that Final Four was going by so fast. You couldn't stop for a moment to appreciate what was happening. Due to the length of time spent with the media, we missed the opportunity

The 1979 national championship game was billed as Magic vs. Bird, but I also got my shot at Larry and he at me. He nailed me in the chest with his shoulder in the first half and nearly knocked me out of the game. But we both finished with 19 points, and I had a career-high nine assists to his two, and that might have been the difference in us winning the title.
*Photo courtesy of Michigan State University*

to hoot and holler with our teammates in the locker room after a tremendous season of accomplishment.

# HUGS AND HANDSHAKES

You'd think that we would have wanted to go out on the town and whoop it up afterward, but when we got back to the hotel, we were thoroughly drained and just kind of gathered in one of our rooms. The load was finally off our backs, and the only way I can explain how we felt is that it was a feeling of relief and, at the same time, utter exhaustion. This thing started way back in Brazil, and we could finally stop running.

Our boosters, parents, and fans were celebrating in one of the big ballrooms in the hotel, and I guess everybody was expecting us to make an appearance, but we had no intention of going down there. The last thing we wanted to do was be around a lot of people. Finally, my dad came up to the room and said, "Hey fellas, there are a lot of people down there who would at least like to greet you and say hello, so why don't you come down for a little while." He was right as usual, so we went and got our pats on the backs and our congratulatory hugs and handshakes. What we really wanted to do was just go back to our rooms and chill, reflect, and savor our one shining moment.

# MEMORIES

Flying home the next day was incredible. When we got on the plane, everybody knew who we were. We had to make a connection in Chicago's O'Hare Airport. During our 90-minute layover we ran into Gino Vanelli, the singer. He and his band had watched the game the night before and we snapped some pictures with him. He took my address along with Earvin's, and Ron Charles', and about three weeks later he sent us a complete collection of his albums. That was great.

When we got back to Lansing, there was a throng waiting for us at the airport, and then we bused right over to Jenison Field House, which was jam-packed. We were basking in celebrity. It was a phenomenal time. I guess I've always been a reflective person and remember thinking to myself that these are moments that you can't grab and hold because they're fleeting. Then they become memories and that's what you've got. Everything you've accomplished becomes a part of history the instant it's done. I think about this every year when a new national champion is crowned.

I'm sure that whenever a person wins a championship, he or she becomes filled with a wonderful feeling of accomplishment. You wish it was something tangible that lasts and lasts so you can actually hold it, touch it, feel it, look at, embrace it . . . , but you can't.

That's what I remember trying to do. It might have hit me differently because I was the only senior on that team, and it was truly over for me. I was trying to capture every single drop of it.

# STANDING TALL
# AMONG GIANTS

We all know how Earvin and Larry went on to save the NBA and become legendary professional players. I'm not saying I was the best player on the floor the night Michigan State beat Indiana State, but if I didn't sit those eight minutes with four fouls, I probably would have had 25 points, 12 assists, and 12 rebounds, and been named the MVP of the Final Four. I know that. It's not lost on me, but I'm okay with that, because we won the game. I didn't care about being MVP. I was the MVP of the Mideast Regional off the Notre Dame game. How many people know it? What would have been different?

Was it one of my best games at Michigan State? When you factor in the magnitude of the game, perhaps it was. But from a purely statistical standpoint, it's not even close. It's hard to ignore the 36-point, 13-rebound game against Notre Dame, or the 36 and 10 against Detroit in a tournament-like atmosphere at Calihan Hall back in '77.

I had many great performances as a Spartan. Nevertheless, putting up 19 points, eight rebounds, and nine assists in a game of such stature, and that going in was overwhelmed by the personas of Larry Bird and Earvin "Magic" Johnson, says something. It really goes along with what I always sought to do, and that's not to get lost in the shadow of anybody.

9

# THE MICHIGAN STATE 79ERS

## AN EVERLASTING BOND

The best thing about our 1979 national championship team was that we all got along. We liked each other and had a lot of fun. We used to crack on each other unmercifully and still do. As great as some of our players were, or how obscure others may have been, talk to any one of them, and he will say being a part of Michigan State's national championship made a significant difference in his life and he enjoys the benefits of it to this day. Even if everything that's said about Coach Heathcote being irascible, curmudgeonly, and demanding is unequivocally true, we knew he always had our best interests at heart and was a benevolent dictator . . . at least some of the time. We will always be connected by an indestructible bond.

## BOBO "NO SWEAT" CHARLES, THE LADY'S MAN

What the character Grady was to the *Sanford and Son* TV show, Ron "Bobo" Charles was to the 1979 national champion Spartans. When he first came to MSU from the Virgin Islands, he was real skinny and had a big Afro that made him look like a Q-tip.

I'm probably the first to ever tell the true story about why we call him Bobo. Don Flowers, a reserve guard on our 1977-78 Big Ten

16

championship team, used the word "bobos" to describe the methods of a guy who was popular with the ladies. Ron Charles was mild-mannered, and the women used to think he was so cute with his Virgin Island accent. But Ron was a sly cat, you might say. We started calling him the "Bobo Man," and that evolved into "Bobo."

One day, Coach Heathcote was getting on Ron in practice and yelled, "Bobo, get your ass going," and everybody cracked up because Coach called him Bobo, and we knew he didn't know what it meant. Lo and behold, one morning in the student paper, *The State News*, there was a photo of Ron blocking a shot accompanied by a caption that referred to him as Ron "Bobo" Charles. He was "Bobo" to everyone from then on.

Just like today's players, we had to have our music, and when we went on our preseason trip to Brazil, Bobo was in charge of providing the tunes. The boom boxes we had back then were huge, and Bobo had one that was as big as a coffee table. Problem was he brought along only one cassette tape, by Ashford & Simpson, to play on it. We couldn't find any American music in the local stores and there were no English-speaking radio stations available, so it was Ashford & Simpson or nothing at all. We listened to that tape over and over and over. Ron assumed we'd bring our own tapes, but hey, he was in charge of the music.

I love Bobo like a brother, and I talk to him the most of all the guys on the team. We shared an apartment, and he's just one of those easy-going guys. He was a terrific talent and one who really sacrificed for the good of the team. He could have starred somewhere else, but on this team he had to take a secondary role. Nevertheless, he flourished as a sixth man and then as a starter. Don Monson, one of Coach Heathcote's assistants, called Ron "No Sweat," because nothing bothered him. He did things so effortlessly, it looked like he was barely working.

## JAY VINCENT, BIG HOMEBODY

We didn't know how easy it was going to be to recruit Jay Vincent until later on when we found out how badly he hated to leave the Lansing-East Lansing area. If Jay could have played all 27 games, the NCAA Tournament and the Final Four in East Lansing, he would have been a happy fella. We'd be on our way to a road game and Jay would say, "Man, I can't wait until we get back," and we hadn't even left the Lansing airport.

Ron "Bobo" Charles went by a number of nicknames, but my good friend was also known as "No Sweat." *Photo courtesy of Michigan State University*

We called him "Big Daddy–Fat Daddy" because he was the biggest guy on the team weight wise, and it seemed like everything associated with him was big. You could count on Jay to order two large milks with every meal regardless of what he was eating. He had a big red van with a huge gray stripe that went around the entire vehicle. It looked like a Buckeyemobile and stood out so much he wasn't hard to find. Sometimes we'd spot Jay's van out and about at 1 a.m., so we also called him the "Midnight Creeper."

The tight short-shorts we wore back then made Jay look pudgier than he actually was. Jay had big, soft hands, unbelievable foot speed, and deceptive quickness. He'd work you over in the post. Despite having a lot of baby fat on him, he could really move and get it going. He'd get you off the floor and out of position so he could score easily with the up-and-unders. He had a bevy of moves, plus he could knock it down from 18 feet. Jay was unstoppable against Illinois his freshman year and was wearing the Illini out so much Eddie Johnson shouted, "Somebody guard that fat pig!" That was one of the funniest things we heard on the court that season.

I always had great compassion for Jay because I think he felt he was playing second fiddle to Earvin Johnson. Heck, we all were, but I think Jay was always trying to prove he was an equally great player. When Jay broke his foot in the tournament, I really felt bad for him because Ron Charles stepped into the void and we didn't miss a beat. I've said this for more than 25 years, and I'm sure I'll keep saying it for as long as I can recall the events of those two seasons—without Jay Vincent we wouldn't have enjoyed the kind of success we did. He was far too important to what we were all about.

# FATEFUL TERRY DONNELLY

Terry Donnelly was the little left-hander who joined the team for the 1976-77 season. He certainly wasn't the best guard on the team and probably should not have been starting as a freshman. At times, it was a mystery why he was in the lineup ahead of Don Flowers and a few others. I came to understand that Coach Heathcote was building for the future, and Don Flowers was not the future—Terry Donnelly was. Terry made his share of mistakes while we compiled a 10-17 record, but by the time he became a junior and was surrounded by Jay, Earvin, and me, he was ready to flourish.

It's funny how things turn out. After our infamous team meeting at a critical point in the 1978-79 season, Coach replaced Terry in the starting lineup with Gerald Busby, a freshman. Busby then inexplicably quit the team, prompting Coach to hold a vote on whether he should make an effort get Busby to change his mind. Well, a majority of hands went up supporting the attempt, but I often wondered if Terry put his hand up. I don't remember seeing it, because Busby being out of the picture secured Terry's spot in the starting lineup. Someday I need to ask Terry, "Hey, man, did you raise your hand?"

Terry also had to settle for a lesser role but became a very good defender, and when the opportunity arose he could shoot the basketball with the best of them. That's why in the national championship game he took advantage of Indiana State not guarding him and knocked down each of his five shots and all but one of six free throws. He had 15 points in the most important game of his life.

# THE GOLDEN ARM

Michael Brkovich is the most unassuming guy I have ever come across. I don't think he ever fully believed in his ability as a basketball player, and he got a scholarship in the weirdest way. He lived in Windsor, Ontario, across the river from Detroit, and in the springtime he'd come to East Lansing to play pick-up basketball with the guys. He dunked on people and shot the ball with tremendous range. I don't think he came to MSU looking for a scholarship; he was just seeking competition. Nevertheless, he was discovered by the coaching staff during that three-month period.

Did Michigan State's fate change when freshman guard Gerald Busby decided to leave the team after being tabbed for his first collegiate start in a pivotal game against Ohio State? Would the Spartans still have gone on to win the national championship if Terry Donnelly (No. 11)—shown here with Coach Heathcote, Earvin, and me after we defeated Notre Dame in the regional final—hadn't gotten his starting job back because of Busby's departure? No wonder Terry, who had a great performance in the national championship game against Indiana State, is smiling. *Photo courtesy of Michigan State University*

Michael earned the nickname "the Golden Arm" because of his flawless jump shot, but we used to have to beg him to shoot the ball. It was the darnedest thing. No one ever had to ask me twice to shoot. You might have to beg me to stop shooting, but Michael was reluctant. Even though he was the best pure shooter in the Big Ten, Coach had to get on him constantly to "shoot the damn ball." One of the best things for Michael and our team was having Earvin on the floor with him because Earvin boosted his confidence. After Earvin got him the basketball you'd hear, "Shoot it, Michael. Shoot it, Michael."

If we had had the three-point line, Michael Brkovich would have averaged 12 to 15 points a game. The game in which I thought he had the most confidence was the regional final against Notre Dame. He opened the game with a dunk that put the Irish back on their heels and went on to finish with 13 points. Michael could be a clutch performer, too, as he demonstrated by hitting the two most important free throws of the year against Iowa with three seconds left in regulation to tie the score and send the game into overtime. It was a game we absolutely had to win, and we did, thanks to him.

Michael Brkovich was a happy-go-lucky guy and a tremendous basketball player who got a college education and earned a starting position on a national championship team off of pick-up basketball.

## THAT'S DR. LONGAKER TO YOU

Michael Longaker was the brains on the team. He studied eight hours a day. He might have studied more than all of us put together because that's all he did. He had this pretty girlfriend named Mary Beth, and we used to kid him all the time that if he didn't start spending some time with her, one of us would. He didn't like that too much. We used to tell him he didn't have to study every minute of the day, but to no avail.

He knew that basketball wasn't going to be his future, but I'm sure his earning power in the medical profession is commensurate with that of many professional athletes. Dr. Longaker is the director of children's surgical research in the Department of Surgery, Division of Plastic, and Reconstructive Surgery, at the Lucile Salter Packard Children's Hospital at Stanford University.

Michael was the voice of reason on our team. Whatever damage Coach had done to your psyche, Michael would be the one who would always come over and try to soothe it. Coach has said that when we had that meeting after the Northwestern blowout, a lot of people said a lot of things, but what made the most sense was Michael saying let's look around the room, be honest with ourselves and accept the fact that we're not playing up to our potential.

# DON BRKOVICH, THE RUSTY ARM

Don Brkovich was Michael's younger brother and a fun guy to have on the team. Donny used to think that because his last name was Brkovich he could shoot, because he didn't hesitate to hoist them. The only problem was, they didn't go in like Michael's did, and he'd get in trouble for it during practice. While Michael's arm was golden, Donny's was often rusty, but he was a good player on our scouting team. Those guys would really go at us in practice and try to make things as difficult as possible for the starters. We couldn't have accomplished what we did without them.

# ROB GONZALEZ

In my estimation, Rob Gonzalez was never the same after Earvin put him in his place during a pick-up game before the 1979 season. Rob and Earvin weren't crazy about each other after that, but they got along. We all got along. Rob felt that coming in as a high school All-American he should be playing significant minutes right away. I later found out that Rob often visited Coach Heathcote's office to tell him he should be in the starting lineup.

Coach would say, "Well Rob, who are you going to play in front of? Do you want me to sit Earvin?"

"No, Earvin's pretty good."

"Should you be playing in front of Jay?"

"No, Jay does a nice job. He's fine."

"You think you should be starting in front of Gregory?"

"Yeah."

I wasn't aware of those conversations until they came to light in Coach's 1995 book, and I must admit I laughed. I guess that's how he was supposed to feel. You've got to believe in yourself. I'm OK with it. Rob transferred to the University of Colorado in 1980 to finish his collegiate career and lives in Mexico City. I've seen him a few times, and he looks great, like he could still play. He just might be able to take that starting spot from me now.

## "JERALD JEEKEE"

I remember reading Gerald Gilkie's name a lot in the newspaper when I played for Detroit Henry Ford High School and Gerald starred for Detroit Kettering. When I first met him at Michigan State, I expected him to be a lot bigger, because when you read so much about somebody you automatically think he's larger than life. Gerald went to Brazil with us, and the public address announcer apparently couldn't pronounce a hard *G*, so he called him "Jerald Jeekee." So that was his name the rest of the season. Gerald was a hard-working guy and a really good teammate.

## GREGORY LLOYD, THE WHIPPING BOY

Gregory Lloyd played at Lansing Eastern High School with Jay, had a really nice senior year, and went to the University of Arizona. Things didn't work out too well there, so he came back and joined our team in 1978. Our nickname for him was "G. Lloyd," and he was a very valuable scouting team guy and a bit of a whipping boy for Coach Heathcote.

Coach often had to rein G. Lloyd in when he executed his own game plan in practice. Coach would tell him, "not your way, our way." Just to give you an idea of how single-minded and consistent Coach is, he picked up where he left off with G. Lloyd during the 10-year anniversary celebration of our national championship season. The centerpiece of the event was a reunion game against a team of other former Spartan greats in Jenison Field House. We were provided uniforms, but no warmups—not that we needed them on that hot

August day. While we were in our lay-up line, G. Lloyd stood out as the only one on either team wearing sweat pants. Now he's 31 years old by then, but there's Coach saying, "Greg, you want to take those damn pants off? You always have to be different." It was ten years later, and Coach was still hounding G. Lloyd. Greg performed well in the game, but he hasn't attended any reunions since.

# HEY KAYE

Rick Kaye did a lot to help me prepare for games. He was a little bit bigger than I was and had little ways of getting under my skin. He knew he could be extremely frustrating and even got perverse satisfaction out of doing whatever he could to throw me off my game in practice. And of course, whenever he did, there was Coach ready to remind me that I was a senior and shouldn't be making such foolish mistakes. Rick enjoyed freedom rarely afforded the starters because Coach's greatest attention was on the first team. Any time the scouting team could make Coach scream at us they loved it, and Rick Kaye seemed to be the ring leader of that group.

# HIGH-FLYING GERALD BUSBY

Gerald Busby arrived as a David Thompson sky-walker type. He was a 6-foot-4 freshman, could really rise and had unbelievable hops and flexibility. He was one of those guys who could lie on his back flat on the floor, kick out both legs and suddenly be standing. He used to amaze us with that. Gerald never really settled in at Michigan State and left the team soon after Coach placed him in the starting lineup prior to our pivotal game against Ohio State. I've seen him once since, and that was at the ten-year anniversary game. He was sitting in the stands, and Earvin pointed him out to me. After leaving MSU, Gerald went on to star at Ferris State in Big Rapids, Michigan, where he scored 1,004 points and pulled down 318 rebounds from 1980 to 1983. He led the Bulldogs to a pair of Great Lakes Intercollegiate Athletic Conference titles and was the league's Player of the Year in '83. I've always wondered how he was able to reconcile leaving our team, given what we accomplished two months later.

# SHOES "BRICKMEISTER" HUFFMAN

Sure, everybody knows Jaimie Huffman as "Shoes" because of how his shoe came off during the NCAA Tournament game against Lamar. As he struggled to get it back on while play continued, NBC color analyst Al McGuire said he'd forever be known as "Shoes" Huffman. But to us, Jaimie Huffman was "Brickmeister." Jaimie was a walk-on who wasn't very good offensively but was scrappy on defense. We called him "The Brickmeister," because every shot he attempted would just clang off the rim. He had no touch whatsoever, and the heaviest shot I ever saw.

He got more publicity from losing a shoe than anything else he ever did in basketball, and fans still remember him fondly to this day. I wonder how many of them know that Jaimie played his high school basketball at Lansing Everett and won a state championship with Earvin Johnson in 1977. Jaimie's basketball resume is impressive with high school, Big Ten, and NCAA titles. Not bad for a Brickmeister.

# "MANAGEMENT!"

Randy Bishop and Darwin Payton were very good student managers, and I give both of them a lot of credit for being able to work for Coach Heathcote, because as we all know he's not the easiest guy in the world to please. Randy by far was the quieter of the two. He did his job and I don't remember him ever complaining.

Now Darwin—he's a different story altogether. I don't think there's ever been a manager like Darwin Payton. He wasn't a player, but he certainly wanted to be treated with the same accord and respect as one. Coach had this thing for calling student aides "management." He'd yell, "Management get over here. Management do this. Management do that." One day, Darwin said, "Coach, my mother didn't name me Management. My name is Darwin." It must have resonated, because Coach called him "Dar" from then on. That was typical Darwin. My nickname for him is "Dar-Baby" and he was in tight with the team. He was close to Earvin, Jay, Bobo, and me. It got to the point where Coach would call Darwin to get a gauge on what we were thinking. And Darwin would tell him, "Coach, I think you need to lighten up on Jay a little bit." He had Coach's ear. I don't think Coach ever had that level respect for a manager before or after.

# BILL BERRY AND DAVE HARSHMAN

I don't know if Coach Berry knew it, but a lot of us had a crush on his wife. Oh my gosh, she was a pretty lady and still is. We loved it when Mrs. Berry would come around. It was no surprise to us when he left to become the head coach at San Jose State, because he was a very good coach and we benefited from his vast basketball knowledge.

Dave Harshman was the son of Marv Harshman, who was Jud Heathcote's mentor and confidant. Dave was young, energetic, and obviously understood the game. He related with so many of us because he was just a few years older than we were. He was very easy to talk to, and we liked him a lot.

# CLINT THOMPSON, TRAINER AND FRIEND

I consider Clint Thompson a friend, because he was a guy you could talk to about anything. He used to always draw out my name, "Gregggg-orrrr-y, you've just got to hang in there. Don't worry so much about what Coach is saying. You can get through it." When I was playing for the Detroit Pistons, Clint helped me a great deal after I hurt my knee. He oversaw my rehab following surgery and helped me regain the strength in my knee. Clint was responsible for me being able to play in the Association for as long as I did.

# ED BELOLI, EQUIPMENT MANAGER

Ageless Ed Beloli was our equipment manager, and he guarded the gear like it was gold. We got one pair of shorts and one jockstrap. One time I cut off my sweatpants to make shorts, and he nearly had a conniption. I had to ask him, "Ed, are you paying for this stuff out of your own pocket?" He was a wonderful man who attended our 25-year reunion, and although he was approaching 90, he looked at least 20 years younger.

# DR. K, ACADEMIC ALL-AMERICAN

Clearly, my most cherished accomplishment at Michigan State is the national championship I shared with my teammates, but there have been other achievements of which I am truly proud. Shortly after being selected All-American in 1979, I was the first Spartan basketball player named to the Academic All-America first team. This caught me totally off guard. It was unbelievable, and I have many people to thank for it. First, my parents, Verna and Walter Kelser, who always emphasized the importance of education and made it very clear that they would always support any athletic endeavors that I chose. However, they also stressed that it was my responsibility to maintain a high standard in the classroom.

I continued to embrace that concept at Michigan State and received tremendous motivation and encouragement from Silas Taylor, who served as my academic adviser. Just as Coach Heathcote pushed for greater effort on the court, Silas urged the same for the classroom. I remember visiting him often at his office, where he had posted a copy of one of his MSU report cards on his bulletin board. I couldn't help but notice three perfect grades of 4.0 and one 3.5. He reminded me that I was capable of doing the same, and I would be cheating myself with anything less. My parents loved Silas, because he echoed what they had always preached.

In 1998 I received a call from then-Michigan State president M. Peter McPherson informing me of the university's decision to present me with an honorary doctorate of humanities degree, and to ask if I would give the commencement address at the spring graduation ceremony. After I picked myself up off the floor, I thanked him and said it would be an incredible honor. This great recognition made every instance of feeling undervalued and overlooked during my athletic career seem less important but a necessary part of the journey, nonetheless. It couldn't get any better than this. I am very grateful to Peter McPherson and his successor, former provost Lou Anna K. Simon, who helped make this possible and remains a dear friend.

Twenty-eight years ago I politely asked people to not call me Dr. K. I now acknowledge that moniker with a great deal of Spartan pride.

# 10

# MY LIFE AND TIMES WITH EARVIN "MAGIC" JOHNSON

## FROM EARVIN TO MAGIC

**W**hen former *Lansing State Journal* sportswriter Fred Stabley Jr. dubbed Earvin "Magic" after one of his phenomenal high school performances, I thought it was cute. But I never call him Magic, and neither did the rest of his teammates at Michigan State and the Los Angeles Lakers. If you hear somebody calling him Magic, chances are they don't know him very well. If you're his teammate, you get beyond the "Magic" persona. To me, he's Earvin. With Coach Heathcote, it was always, "EEEEEEEEEEEEE!" The Lakers called him "Buck," for young buck, because he entered the NBA as a 20-year-old rookie.

## A BLESSING ALL THE WAY AROUND

That said, the nickname "Magic" is appropriate in every way for him. While he was a great, great player—let's make no mistake about that—certain things fell into place for him in ways that were almost magical. He took a chance on a Michigan State team that had a losing record instead of the more powerful Michigan program that was coming off a Big Ten championship in 1977. During Earvin's two seasons with the Spartans, the two teams reversed roles, as MSU won back-to-back conference crowns and a national title while U-M sunk to the middle of the pack.

When Earvin declared for the NBA draft, he was considered the top prospect coming out, even though he was just a sophomore. The No. 1 player in the draft usually goes to one of the worst teams, not to a championship contender. And yet things came together seamlessly for Earvin when the Lakers won a coin flip with the Chicago Bulls for the right to draft first in 1979.

He left MSU to join a Lakers team that already had Kareem Abdul-Jabbar, Norm Nixon, and Jamaal Wilkes, and was poised to win a championship. With the addition of Earvin, the Lakers dominated the league for the next ten years. Would he have had similar success in Chicago if the Bulls had won that coin flip? There was no question about whether Earvin was going to be great and that he would win NBA championships, but predicting that the Chicago Bulls would have had five titles in nine years the way the Lakers did might have been a bit optimistic even with him in their lineup. Maybe the Lakers were his reward for taking a chance on Michigan State when, on paper, Michigan appeared to have the stronger program. It's as if the basketball gods said you trusted us on MSU, so we'll give you LA on the pro side.

Earvin has been wonderfully blessed, but so have all of us who have ever been able to call him a teammate. We were blessed to have a once-in-a-generation player's time coincide with our own. In the two years I played with Earvin at Michigan State, we compiled a record of 51-11, and he helped me, and so many others, become a champion. While my scoring average dropped from 22 to 18 points the year Earvin arrived, my shooting accuracy went from 49 percent to 61. That was all Earvin, getting me the ball in the right place at the right time. He made it a lot easier, that's for sure.

# A PREVIEW OF
# THE MAGIC TO COME

In the months after Earvin signed his tender for MSU, he often would come to Jenison Field House to play in the pick-up games that on any given night would feature returning veterans, former Spartans, and NBA players. One time Earvin played in an AAU tournament and sustained a cut between the middle two fingers on his right hand. If you look at it today you can still see scars from where the wound had to be stitched. Anyway, he wasn't supposed to be playing, but you just hated to miss those games because they were so competitive and a lot of fun. When you're 17 years old, you live to play as much as you can. So he came over that one day with his hand heavily wrapped and was unable to use it at all, but that didn't stop him.

Earvin Johnson possessed a unique combination of size, athleticism, power, court savvy, awareness, instinct, work ethic, and competitive drive that may never be matched. *Photo courtesy of Michigan State University*

He not only played, he dominated using only his left hand. He was ball-handling with his left, he was making baby hooks with his left, beating guys off penetration, and finishing with his left. It was an unforgettable display. He ended one game by taking a little lefty jumper from 14 feet, and I said to myself, "He is truly special." You don't have to be a person with a lot of wisdom and experience to recognize when greatness is in your midst. I became aware of it very quickly and used to tell people this guy was advanced beyond his years. This was May of 1977. Earvin was still only 17 years old and hadn't graduated from high school yet.

# MAKING A POINT

Coach Heathcote started off playing Earvin in the frontcourt. And really, throughout the 62 games he played as a Spartan, Earvin was always in the frontcourt on defense, but handled the ball almost exclusively on offense. Our lineup during Earvin's first year consisted of guards Bob Chapman, Terry Donnelly, Earvin, Jay Vincent, and me in the frontcourt. The second year ended with Terry and Michael Brkovich as the guards, and Ron "Bobo" Charles or Jay, and Earvin, and me on the front line.

# TONE DEAF

As gifted as Earvin was, he couldn't do everything well. For example, he thought he could sing. The group Enchantment had a song called, "It's You that I Need." He would take his normal seat at the back of the bus bound for a morning shootaround before a road game, hair uncombed, still with a little frog in his throat, trying to sing, "It's You That I Need," which called for some pretty high vocals that he didn't have. I would tell Earvin, it's certainly not *you* that I need. I think I spoke for everyone, because he was terrible.

# AN OBSESSIVE COMPETITOR

Earvin wanted to win at everything and would do everything in his power to prevail in cards, checkers, backgammon, or basketball. It didn't matter. Winning had to be the end result. This is going to seem extremely bizarre in this electronic age of Playstation2, Xbox, and iPods; but Jay Vincent carried a checkerboard with him on road trips and was the self-proclaimed Checkermaster. He beat most everybody on the team with the exception of Earvin and me, because we chose not to play him. But one day, Earvin got his fill of Jay bragging about his prowess at checkers and decided to take him on. The game took about 45 minutes, because Earvin was deliberate with every single move. Making Jay wait was Earvin's way of taking him out of his comfort zone. Needless to say, we were all pulling for Earvin because we had also had enough of Jay's loud talk. Sure enough, Earvin took down the Checkermaster. If it took dragging the game out forever to unnerve Jay and win at checkers, then he was willing to do that. Footnote: We never saw that checkerboard again after Earvin's victory.

We became very good friends, but I realized that with Earvin it's all about winning, and you can't take things personally. He was not averse to screaming at guys if they weren't doing what was necessary to win. One time at Illinois in 1977-78 we were winning late in the game, and I tried to salt it away with a hook shot. He immediately got on me, "Greg, don't take that shot." It kind of caught me off guard because I was a junior and he was a freshman and had never done anything like that before. I thought it was a great shot, but he didn't because there was no shot clock and it didn't have to be taken. After the game, I went up to him and said, "What was your problem?"

He said, "I was just trying to win the game."

We let it go and that's the only time he ever did that, and I'm sure I took far worse shots than that one in the games that followed.

When I played with the Seattle SuperSonics in the NBA, we played Earvin's Lakers six times each year. I remember in one game I was whistled for a foul I didn't agree with and slammed the ball down on the floor. Earvin turned to the referee and shouted, "Tech, tech, tech." He wanted the ref to hit me with a technical foul. One of my teammates on the bench said to me, "Hey, I thought he was your boy." Once the heat of competition dissipated after the game, Earvin and I went out to dinner. He was unparalleled at being friends off the court and being a cold-blooded competitor on the court.

Earvin is a competitor of the highest order, and winning comes before friendship. Once I understood that when we hit the court we weren't friends, it was fun, it was cool.

# BEST PLAYER, HARDEST WORKER

Earvin spent countless hours working on his game and the various things he needed to do to get better. He was a superb ball-handler, and you could not take the ball away from him, but he worked on it all the time. He always played hard in practice, as did I, because practice carries over to the game. During those two years at MSU, the other players had no choice but to work hard and give it all they had because of what Earvin, one of the best players in the entire nation, and I were doing. Earvin was so talented that he made things look easy, but a lot of hard work went into it. In the NBA, he spent each summer working hard in order to add something new to his game.

I can't imagine there ever being a more competitive athlete—in any sport—than Earvin Johnson. I found out just how determined Earvin was to win when we faced each other in the NBA. Our friendship ceased to exist once we were inside the four black lines, although I wanted to beat him just as badly as he wanted to beat me.
*Photo courtesy of Michigan State University*

# REINVENTING THE DUNK

The NCAA brought the dunk back to college basketball in 1976-77, and I took full advantage of it as a sophomore. When Earvin arrived the following season, I was able to take it to new heights, so to speak. Our signature play was the alley-oop—Earvin would throw a lob pass, and I'd slam it through. It was a spectacular and crowd-pleasing way to finish a fast break.

A lot of people credit us for inventing the alley-oop, but we didn't. We were just able to put a bigger exclamation mark at the end of it, leading many to believe we were the first to use it.

# MORE THAN A SMILE

Earvin was always dazzling. First of all, he was 6-foot-9 and still able to handle the basketball, and that made him an oddity right there. Then there were his no-look passes, and pushing the ball up the floor, and his enthusiasm. Put it all together and it gave him just wonderful entertainment value and theater.

Earvin made things easier for everybody he played with. I was an excellent player before Earvin ever got to MSU, and the numbers validate it. While my overall personal statistics went down slightly after he arrived, the number of wins almost tripled.

After Earvin and I left Michigan State, Jay Vincent won two Big Ten scoring crowns as he exploded from 13 points a game as a sophomore to 22 in each of his last two seasons, but the Spartans had losing records in each of those two seasons. I am sure Jay would have traded some of those points for more victories. You see, it really is about winning.

Kareem Abdul-Jabbar won one NBA title, scored more than 20,000 points, and was headed for the Hall of Fame before Earvin got to the Lakers. But when Earvin got there, he made it easier for Kareem, who became an even more prolific winner in addition to being a great player.

# WAS THERE EVER A CHANCE EARVIN WOULD RETURN FOR HIS JUNIOR SEASON?

I was concerned about Earvin leaving after his sophomore season, because I cared deeply about Michigan State, but I felt winning the national championship would be it for him. Earvin came to Michigan State to hone his skills so he could become a professional basketball player. That was his dream, that was his goal, that was his ambition, and he was clearly ready for the NBA. If by chance we had won the national championship in '78, Earvin might have left after only one season.

Jay Vincent, Ron Charles, Terry Donnelly, and Michael Brkovich very much wanted Earvin to return, because if he did, MSU would have been ranked No. 1 in the country entering the 1979-80 season. I was the only departing senior, and Coach Heathcote almost certainly would have been able to sign some of the fine players MSU ultimately lost out on when Earvin decided to leave.

A lot of key recruits were waiting just to see what Earvin was going to do. Michigan State was high on Vern Flemming's list, but all he did is lead Georgia to the 1983 Final Four and play for the 1984 gold-medal-winning U.S. Olympic team. James Worthy grew up in North Carolina, but he waited to see what was going to happen with Earvin before deciding to become a Tar Heel. Whenever I run into Worthy, we always share a laugh over his decision not to come to Michigan State. "Hey man," Worthy says, "you were gone, Earv was gone. I couldn't go there after that." Even Virginia's Ralph Sampson, a three-time college player of the year, had committed to making a visit to MSU. You might think it should have been easy for Coach Heathcote to capitalize on the national championship, but Michigan State's recruiting took a major hit because those guys wanted to play with Earvin. If he would have stayed, Michigan State would have been heavily favored to win another championship, but it was not to be.

# STORM CLOUDS OVER EAST LANSING

I'll never forget the day Earvin announced his decision. It was on a Friday morning at a press conference held at the University Club. I was there along with Coach Heathcote, Ron, and Jay. When we went inside, it was a beautiful, bright, sunshiny day. After Earvin told the gathering of media and onlookers that he was going to become a Los Angeles Laker, we went outside, and unbelievably, within an hour, it was as though we were in the midst of a total eclipse. It got dark and ominous and the rain began to pour down. It was as though a pall came over the City of East Lansing after his decision became known. It was clearly the dawning of a dark period for Michigan State, but not for Earvin. He had accomplished what he went there to do—win a championship, get better, and move up to the next level.

# COMING TO TERMS

By the fall of 1991, my playing days were long over, and I was beginning my seventh year as a sportscaster. On Thursday November 7, I was in Denver preparing to make my debut as the color commentator for Minnesota Timberwolves telecasts on Prime Sports Network. I went to a production meeting late that morning and then went back to my hotel room to do a little studying and take a nap, which was always my routine when I played. While I was dozing, I got a phone call from my wife, Donna, and she asked, "Have you heard the news?" Well, any time somebody says that, you start to worry. Then she said, "I just heard on the television that Earvin is retiring because he's got the AIDS virus." And I was like, "What?!"

I turned the television on, and sure enough, there it was scrolling across the screen, "press conference later today." I was glued to the set. At that time, not everyone was educated on what it meant, and when you heard AIDS, you associated it with a quick deterioration of the body and ultimately death.

When the press conference came on, I remember being surprised by his earnest and upbeat demeanor. Earvin looked good and strong, but I was still very fearful. That night before the game, there was a moment of silence for Earvin as part of a league-wide observance. That made things even more surreal because a moment of silence is usually reserved for someone who has passed away. The gist of it was Magic Johnson had retired and please pray for his health.

The next morning I flew to Sacramento, where the Timberwolves were playing Saturday night. When I got off the plane there were a couple of reporters waiting to interview me. I talked to Earvin later that day and just told him, "Hey man, I am praying for you and hope everything works out. Just hang in there." Again, he was very upbeat. He said he'd be back in Michigan for Thanksgiving and he and Cookie, his wife, would pay us a visit around that time. He appeared on the *Arsenio Hall Show* that night and talked about his situation.

I flew home on Sunday, and when I walked into my office my answering machine was full with at least 50 messages from various reporters wanting my thoughts on Earvin. I was really glad I was out of town when the news was breaking. Earvin and Cookie came to visit the day after Thanksgiving and had dinner with Donna and me and my old friend Phil Hubbard and his wife, Jackie. We had a wonderful evening, and it felt no different than any other time we had all been together.

Since then, of course, we have learned that Earvin does not have AIDS, but is HIV-positive. I applaud and admire the way he has gone about his life in the usual Earvin way—thinking like a winner. I don't know how many other people would have been able to do that. I don't know if I could. He has approached this challenge with the same intensity and fortitude he has always demonstrated when chasing a goal. Here it is 15 years later, and when you see or think of Earvin Johnson, HIV isn't the first thing that comes to mind, or even the second or third.

Earvin had been a superstar athlete in Hollywood—young, rich, attractive, charismatic. He was doing what many have done before, and many still do—he was living his life as a bachelor in the land of stars. I wasn't surprised by his highly publicized lifestyle, and I didn't once make any judgments. I had compassion and understanding. The only surprise was that he had that "Magic" moniker, and everything always seemed to fall into place for him, and yet he could be hit with this just like anyone else. It also didn't surprise me that he turned this tragedy into a positive. Many other people who could not make a difference have been afflicted with HIV. When Earvin "Magic" Johnson contracted the virus, it positioned him to make a positive impact in the fight against this terrible disease, and the one he's made has been sizeable.

# 11

# JUD

## A SINGULAR INDIVIDUAL

You know someone has reached a lofty status when they can get through life with only one name. That's how it is with Coach Heathcote, who I still can't, out of respect and gratitude, refer to only as "Jud"—except when he's not in the room. He was and always will be "Coach Heathcote" to me, even if he's just "Jud" to everybody else.

Coach could be so tough on you and wear you down, but I say that with affection, because I would play for Jud Heathcote again. Aside from everything that may have occurred when I was playing for him, and as tough as he made it sometimes, I have the utmost respect for him and appreciate him and the influence he has had on my life. Coach often demonstrated that he cared about me as a person and not just an athlete.

## MAKING THE GRADE

Although I was an Academic All-American when I left MSU as the No. 1 draft choice of the Detroit Pistons, I was still 26 credits away from graduating with a bachelor's degree in criminal justice. The shortfall occurred because I had arranged my class load in a way that had allowed me to get the very best grades possible while still devoting maximum energy and effort to basketball. I had also elected not to attend summer school so that I could get a job and continue to work on

Everybody knows who you're talking about if you refer to Michigan State's basketball coach named Jud. *Photo courtesy of Michigan State University*

my game. I hadn't been overly concerned, because I had intended to complete my degree requirements, but I can't tell you how many times Coach called me and said, "When are you going to get your butt back here and finish?" I was in no hurry and could have done it after my pro career. However, I went back after my rookie year and completed 13 credits, and after my second year I earned the rest because of his badgering me. Coach attended the commencement ceremony on June 14, 1981, as Terry Donnelly, Gerald Gilkie, and I received our diplomas. While I wasn't playing for Coach Heathcote anymore, and my graduating meant nothing to his next Spartan team, he encouraged me to finish what I had started without further procrastination.

Obviously, Coach helped me become a better basketball player as well. He forced me to think about the game and pay attention to detail. I've often told people that Coach taught me to understand where the "good enough" line is, and why it's important to go beyond it. Just as I would want to play for Coach again, I hope that he would want to coach me again.

# JUD AND GUS

Both of my Spartan coaches were tough, strong-minded taskmasters; however, their styles and personalities were on opposite ends of the universe. Gus Ganakas was a natty dresser, charming and positive, while Jud Heathcote was unconcerned with fashion, coarse, and negative. Somehow, the man MSU unceremoniously fired and the man who took his job are inexplicably wonderful friends.

I don't know when their friendship started. I'd have to imagine it was extremely hard for Coach Ganakas at the beginning, and maybe even during that second year when we started winning big with players that he had brought to MSU. Furthermore, popular opinion suggests that Earvin Johnson most assuredly would have signed with MSU to play for Coach Ganakas, while the coaching change put that eventuality in jeopardy.

Coach Ganakas could have made life rough for Coach Heathcote by being publicly critical, especially during that first year when we had a losing record after five straight winning seasons. But that wasn't Coach Ganakas. Coach Heathcote could have made things miserable for Coach Ganakas by ostracizing him and taking credit for developing his "players." But, that wasn't Coach Heathcote. Instead, they played golf together and were both "the bigger man" about the situation. I've always been truly thankful and appreciative of Coach Heathcote for embracing Coach Ganakas—at whatever point it occurred—because I think it meant a lot to him to be accepted and re-welcomed, so to speak.

# WORD TO THE WISE—DON'T MESS WITH A CONTROL FREAK

Under Coach Ganakas, when we were on the road we ate meals as a team, and each guy ordered whatever he wanted off the menu. No big deal. That luxury vanished under Coach Heathcote. We had an incident in Bloomington, Indiana, during my sophomore year on the morning before we were to play the defending national champion Hoosiers. Coach Heathcote did the ordering for everybody—scrambled eggs, bacon, hash browns, toast, and iced tea. Well, I probably wanted pancakes, but I had to eat toast because Coach says so? At one point,

Coach Heathcote left the room and we all wanted orange juice so we ordered four pitchers and had them put it on the bill. Around two o'clock that afternoon, he called a team meeting and said, "Who the hell ordered this orange juice?"

No one would say anything.

"Dammit, who ordered this orange juice?" Coach said.

So I said, "Coach, we wanted orange juice, so we ordered some."

"I'll tell you what," Coach snapped back. "You guys are going to pay for it."

The orange juice cost around $29, and we had to come up with what was a lot of money in 1977—and still is—for poor college students. We each threw in about three or four dollars apiece to pay for this orange juice. We were so angry, and I was thinking, "This guy's a dictator. This is crazy." But it galvanized us enough that we went out and beat the Hoosiers on their home floor, although Kent Benson was the only starter back from their national title team.

## COACH HEATHCOTE GETS HIS COMEUPPANCE

Our return from the 1978 Far West Classic in Portland, Oregon, took three days thanks to a snowstorm. When we finally made it back to Detroit Metropolitan Airport on January 2, our luggage wasn't coming out fast enough at baggage claim for Coach Heathcote, who is a notoriously impatient traveler. The conveyor belt was moving, but nothing was on it. "What the hell is taking so long?" Coach fumed. Taking matters into his own hands, Coach jumped aboard the conveyor belt and disappeared through one of the chutes. We waited for a few minutes for him to come out of the other chute, but he never did. Instead, he was escorted through a security door by a couple of uniformed officers. That's the first time I had ever seen Coach Heathcote's furor come up zeroes. Coach intimidated everybody from bus drivers to game officials to staff to his assistant coaches, but he couldn't intimidate those officers. They weren't moved at all, and he didn't make our luggage come out any faster either.

# ALIENATING THE DETROIT PUBLIC SCHOOL LEAGUE

Coach coached his way, and at times, intimidation had been enough to motivate us. He'd get in your face, always stay on your case, and push, push, push all the time. He also recruited his way, and that's why I feel during his 19 years at MSU he never really made a recruiting dent in the Detroit Public School League. He wasn't going to go out and kowtow to any 17- or 18-year-old kid. That wasn't his style. He wasn't kissing anybody's butt nor would he acquiesce to any of the high school coaches in Detroit or anywhere else.

Coach wasn't one to compromise his beliefs, and sometimes that approach caused him to lose kids—that's what happened with the PSL. I think in his 19 years, he signed three, maybe four, kids out of the Detroit public schools—Patrick Ford, Steve Smith, and Kevin Willis by way of Jackson (Michigan) Community College. I was already there, so don't count me. The number of standout players he didn't get out of Detroit is enormous. The fact that he did not endear himself to PSL may have inhibited him from achieving even greater success.

# CROSSING THE LINE

I had always considered myself a coachable guy who could be criticized, yelled and screamed at, and even belittled within the confines of the team. There was one incident my junior year when Coach took things beyond the team, and it was incredibly embarrassing for me.

Each year, Coach put on a basketball clinic that was always well attended by coaches from all over the Midwest, fans, and casual observers. One of our practices was included in the program, and while we went through our drills he explained coaching techniques with the aid of a microphone.

For some reason he chose that day to just beat me up during an intrasquad scrimmage. He ripped me up and down the boards, while speaking into the mike in front of all those people. I considered just sitting down for the rest of practice but said, "No, I'm not going to do that, I'm going to weather this."

As soon as practice was over I asked him for a meeting in his office. I got my shower and went up to see him. I was 20 years old but said, "Coach, what happened today cannot happen again. You had that microphone and you were on my case constantly. It was embarrassing. You know I have always been coachable. I accept your criticism and have never disrespected you, but Coach, what you did in front of all those people is unacceptable. I cannot take that."

He responded by going over my mistakes and why he felt he had to point them out. He didn't apologize, but I think that day I gained a measure of respect from Coach Heathcote. I didn't give it back to him and attempt to show him up in front of everyone like I could have or maybe even wanted to. I used the opportunity to meet with him man-to-man. I was calm, explained myself, and just let him know that within the team structure, whatever he wanted to do was fine. But in a situation like that, it's totally unacceptable. "I'm a man, just like you are," I said. Coach never did anything like that again, and I began to feel like finally he was looking at me not as a child, but as a rapidly maturing young adult. That stands out in my mind as the point where my relationship with Coach Heathcote took a turn for the better.

# A MASTER TACTICIAN

Coach Heathcote can break a team down to its very core. His game prep was outstanding, and we knew everything we could expect from the other team. We never lost a game because we were caught by surprise by something. We may not have played well, shot well, or defended well, but it wasn't because we weren't prepared.

I still have his playbook on the high-low offense and all its variations. It's as thick as a phone book and would work splendidly in today's game. You hear about Detroit Pistons coach Flip Saunders and his multioptioned calls, where one play has five possibilities. Coach Heathcote's plays were like that. There were a lot of different contingences, and if the first option didn't work, we would morph right into something else. That's why we were tough for teams to handle defensively man-to-man. Coach also allowed us to free flow, especially after we got Earvin. Giving guys the freedom to do what they do best takes a certain amount of trust, because it requires a coach to live with mistakes. Now Coach may not have been the greatest at living with our errors, but over time we earned his trust.

Earvin used to take a variety of unorthodox shots where he'd be hanging in the air—suspension shots, leaners in the lane, runners, and jump shots off one foot. Most coaches would say, "Don't do that," but Coach allowed it with one caveat. He'd say, "Eeeeeee, if you're going to take those shots, then you have to practice them." So Coach would work on those off-balance shots with Earvin after practice. Sometimes we'd laugh while watching Earvin contort and grimace against imaginary defenders.

# ALWAYS TRUE TO HIMSELF

Coach is brutally honest and doesn't worry much about how that makes you feel. He's never going to change. In the summer of 2000, Coach was scheduled to speak to a large group in Lansing, and they called me to introduce him. I said it would be an honor to present Coach. There were about 600 people in attendance, and I told them wonderful stories about Coach and the impact he's had on my life. I concluded my address by saying, "It gives me great pleasure to present my coach, Jud Heathcote."

Coach took the podium, said, "Thank you, Gregory," and went into his stand-up routine, which the crowd thoroughly enjoyed. When things turned serious Coach began his speech, one he said he had given on many occasions. The speech was about the four favorite players in his 25-year coaching career. He started off with Eric Hays, who played for him at Montana in the early '70s. He spoke about Eric's work ethic and how he became a great player despite lacking outstanding ability. Michael Ray Richardson, who also played at Montana, was the next player Coach talked about. He spoke of his close relationship with Michael Ray, and how difficult it was to leave him to take the Michigan State job.

Former Spartan great Scott Skiles was the next favorite player on Coach's list. Anyone familiar with MSU basketball knows how fond Coach is of Scott, who in 1985-86 had what remains the most prolific single-season scoring performance of any Spartan since Terry Furlow in 1975-76.

Of course we all knew who the last player on the list was going to be. Coach said Earvin "Magic" Johnson is his most favorite player of all time. He told a few stories about their time together as coach and player, their relationship, and how they stay in touch.

Afterward, people came up to me and said, "Greg, I was sure you'd be on that list." I had to laugh, because while I knew I was one of Coach's favorite players, I'm not in the top four. Folks thought Coach would include me, at least out of courtesy, because I was there and had introduced him. But no. If you know Coach like I know Coach, he wasn't going to alter or compromise that which he truly felt. Hey, I'm in some select company, because Steve Smith didn't make that list, nor did Shawn Respert, Eric Snow, or big Mike Peplowski.

By the way, I'm putting the finishing touches on a speech called, "My Favorite Coaches." I'm saving it for when Coach is in the audience. It will include Gus Ganakas, Tom Izzo, Lenny Wilkins, and Ben Kelso. Before leaving the stage, I may mention Coach Heathcote, but only as an afterthought.

Just kidding. Truth be told, he'd be prominent on *my list*.

## DAPPER JUD

Coach didn't exactly have an eye for fashion, and his green game-day sport coats are legendary. But when I picture him in my mind, he's wearing those green and white Pro Keds sneakers, green warmup pants, and a tan topcoat down to his knees as he goes out into the cold winter night.

Jud Heathcote's coaching tree has branches reaching across the country. This 1995 photo shows Coach Heathcote flanked by former assistants Stan Joplin (far left), who is now the head coach at Toledo; Tom Izzo, who succeeded him at MSU; Jim Boylen, who after 13 years in the NBA is back at MSU as Izzo's chief assistant; and Brian Gregory, the head coach at Dayton.
*Photo courtesy of Michigan State University*

# 12

# THE NBA: WHAT WAS AND WHAT MIGHT HAVE BEEN

## A LOTTERY PICK, IN A MANNER OF SPEAKING

I went from winning the national championship to, by today's standards, winning the National Basketball Association Lottery. The league didn't start drawing lots to determine the teams making the first seven picks until 1985, and expanded the draw to nine in '89, 11 in '90, 13 in '95, and 14 in 2004. I was the No. 1 pick of the Detroit Pistons and the fourth overall in 1979. When I signed my contract for $1 million over five years, one of the Detroit papers wrote, "It was one of the sweetest deals ever in these parts—all guaranteed." How about that? That amount would be dwarfed 10 years later and considered miniscule by today's top players.

In attendance with me at the NBA Draft in New York were Earvin Johnson, who was taken first by the Los Angeles Lakers, UCLA's David Greenwood who was drafted second by the Chicago Bulls, San Francisco's Bill Cartwright, selected third by the New York Knicks, and Arkansas' Sidney Moncrief, Milwaukee's pick at the fifth slot.

My NBA career was a dream come true, even though it had its trying moments. I'll never forget being consoled by Mrs. Johnson,

Earvin's mother, when the Pistons took me. She said, "Baby, it's going to be OK." I was going to a Pistons team that won 30 games under first-year coach Dick Vitale in 1978-79, and Earvin was bound for the Lakers, who instantly became a championship favorite with him in the fold.

There was serious talk that the defending NBA champion Seattle Supersonics, who owned the sixth and seventh picks, were planning to select me if I was still available. Even though their picks were lower than where I was selected, I would not have minded, because I had gone through the rebuilding process in high school and college. I really enjoyed winning my last two years at MSU and wanted to stay a winner. I felt confident I could go into Seattle and contribute right away. I was probably wrong in thinking that, because Vinnie Johnson, who was a very good player out of Baylor and went to Seattle three picks after me, could not crack the line-up. I don't know if that was so much Vinnie as it was Seattle coach Lenny Wilkins, who wasn't big on playing rookies.

After becoming the No. 1 draft pick of the Detroit Pistons in 1979, I signed a contract one newspaper called, "one of the sweetest deals ever in these parts." Although it would pale in comparison with today's standards, I was pretty proud of it, as were my father and mother, Walter and Verna, seated on my right. Despite my signing, former Pistons coach Dick Vitale (far left in stripes) might have already been contemplating a phenomenally successful career in broadcasting. The Pistons fired him 12 games into the season.
*Photo courtesy of Michigan State Uiversity*

# ON TO THE PISTONS AND DICK VITALE

I remained positive about being taken by Detroit, because getting to the NBA was a goal realized. If I had to go to a team that was struggling, I figured I'd help turn things around as quickly as we did at Michigan State. I knew that Pistons center Bob Lanier was aging and wearing down, but we eventually got Bob McAdoo, so I went into it with an open mind and a lot of optimism. I felt we could be a good team.

I knew Dick Vitale a little bit from when he was at the University of Detroit and recruited me at Detroit Henry Ford High School, but I didn't know what to expect from him as a coach, plus I missed rookie camp because I hadn't signed my contract yet. Before training camp started, I got a curious call from fellow Pistons first-rounder Roy Hamilton out of UCLA. He said, "I just hope you're in shape." Fortunately I was, because I needed to be. Vitale ran the toughest training camp I had ever been a part of. We had two-a-day practices for almost a month, and they seemed to go on forever. He ran a lot of drills like those you see on a football field. We had to high-step through tires and weave around stationary objects as though we were trying to avoid being tackled. It was rough. The Spartan Mile would have been a piece of cake compared to what Vitale had us doing.

# THE GLASS WAS MORE THAN HALF EMPTY

Adversity set in immediately. We won three of our first four games, then lost seven of our next eight and were 4-8. Pistons management fired Dick Vitale, and made his assistant, Richie Adubato, head coach even though he was very inexperienced. So we had to deal with change right away. Bob Lanier went down with an injury and then asked to be traded because he didn't want to be part of a rebuilding effort. We had five rookies and two second-year guys on the team, and then Bob McAdoo got hurt, and John Shumate, who had been starting, was cut. We went from rebuilding to starting over from scratch, and our chances for success were stripped away very quickly. Expansion teams have more experience than we did. We weren't going anywhere.

It's extremely tough knowing before you take the floor that if you play your absolute best, it still probably won't be good enough to win. That's what we dealt with the entire year. We didn't have the experience or the manpower to be competitive in the NBA. Even while losing, you try your best to play team basketball. It's a constant challenge to stay within that framework, but I did it by averaging 14 points and 5.5 rebounds. Unfortunately, I missed a number of games because of that high-ankle sprain they didn't know about back then. In the last 30 games, I averaged 19 points, really played well, and was named to the second-team all-rookie squad, but the Pistons finished with a franchise-worst 16-66 record.

## PISTONS CONTINUE TO MISS ON ALL CYLINDERS

Scotty Robertson was the coach my second year with the Pistons, but we were no better as a team, because our roster did not improve. It fact, it probably got a little bit worse. Individually I got off to a great start. Through the first 10 games, I was starting, averaging 22 points and beginning to establish myself as a solid NBA scorer. But then my knee started to give me major problems, and the medical staff couldn't figure out what to do. I found myself playing three minutes here, five minutes there, just trying to give it a go, but I couldn't do it. I played one game against the Philadelphia 76ers with an electronic stimulating device on my knee. I was wrapped from below my knee all the way up to my hip, and when 76ers coach Billy Cunningham saw that, the first five plays of the game were for Dr. J, who I was guarding that night. I couldn't stay with him and sat down after four minutes. My average declined to 12.3 points per game. That was real disappointing, and then I was traded for the first time.

## TRADES AND INTRIGUE, NBA STYLE

Detroit sent me to the Seattle Supersonics in December of 1980 for a first-round draft pick. When I got out there, I flunked the physical, which Seattle knew was going to happen all along. The Sonics wanted to keep me in the organization and rehab my knee, but only if they could redo the deal and get their No. 1 pick back in exchange for lesser compensation. The Pistons didn't bite, so I was sent back to Detroit on the basis of failing my physical. I was back with a team that tried to trade me and was clearly moving in a new direction. It was difficult to stay positive, and in February of 1981 I had season-ending surgery after playing in just 25 games of a dismal 21-61 campaign.

That's when I went back to Michigan State and finished my requirements for graduation. While there, MSU trainer Clint Thompson helped me rehabilitate my knee in the hopes of being strong enough for my third NBA season.

## FATE DEALS A TOUGH HAND

In an effort to test the progress of my knee during the off-season, I played in the Los Angeles Summer League and averaged 20 points a game. Upon returning to Detroit, I really felt ready to make a big comeback. I was joined in training camp by Isiah Thomas and Kelly Tripucka, who were drafted by then-general manager Jack McCloskey, and it appeared we were poised to compete. I played really well in camp and was confident I was winning the small forward spot when we played Earvin Johnson and the Los Angeles Lakers in an exhibition game at Michigan State's Jenison Field House. It was an exciting game, and my shot that would have tied the score at the buzzer was just long and bounced off the rim. The Lakers won by three points, but I had 20 points.

I played even better in the rematch a few days later at Joe Louis Arena in downtown Detroit. As fate would have it, I drove the lane to attempt a shot over Kareem Abdul-Jabbar in the later stages of the game. Kareem used to block shots by jumping off one leg and then moving forward instead of going straight up. He almost always avoided contact, but this time his knee hit me squarely in the hip and I suffered a hip pointer.

After that, I had to decide if I should play through the injury in the last two exhibition games. Although hip pointers aren't that serious and take only about a week to heal, they are extremely painful. Even something like a sneeze causes you to gasp. Scotty Robertson made it easy when he told me he knew what I could do, and that instead of playing I should take some time off and get well for the season opener. In the meantime, Kelly Tripucka started and played well, and when the season began, he was in the starting lineup and I was coming off the bench. I was very disappointed because Scotty led me to believe that the starting job was mine. If that wasn't the case, I would never have sat out the remaining preseason games.

## A TRADE OF DESTINY

Eleven games into the 1981-82 season I was traded to Seattle, this time for real, in exchange for Vinnie Johnson. I did not want to be traded because it was obvious that the Pistons were ready to turn the corner, and I wanted to be a part of it when it happened. After all, I suffered through a 16-win season with the franchise, probably played too much on a bad knee and had undergone surgery. I figured I was due. We were bringing in better players, and I looked forward to winning again.

Instead, Vinnie Johnson, along with Isiah Thomas and Bill Laimbeer, who was acquired later that season, formed the nucleus of the "Bad Boy" Piston teams that won back-to-back championships in '89 and '90.

## NEVER AGAIN
## AT FULL STRENGTH

My knee was healthy enough to pass my physical and stay with Seattle this time, but I was never close to 100 percent again. I even thought the Sonics might trade me, because I spent the first five games of my third season glued to the bench and couldn't understand why. I eventually became a role player under Coach Lenny Wilkins and finished with my worst year ever at any level—4.9 points and 3.1 rebounds per game. The only consolation was that for the first time in my short NBA career, I was on a team that won more games than it lost. We finished the year 52-30 and made it into the second round of the playoffs.

My happiest days as a pro were spent with the Seattle Supersonics. Even though I was a role player, I demonstrated I could score on anybody—as I am here against Utah's Jeff Wilkins. *Photo courtesy of Michigan State University*

# HAVING FUN AND PROSPERING IN AN UNACCUSTOMED ROLE

The 1982-83 season, my fourth in the league, was a new beginning for me. I spent the entire off-season working hard to get healthy. When I joined the Sonics for training camp, I was in tremendous shape. My knee felt as good as ever since my surgery, and I was able to show Coach Wilkins that I was ready to make a significant contribution. I started the season as the sixth man, and we jumped out to a 12-0 start. Man, was that fun. Nothing beats winning.

I was playing 20 minutes a game, averaged eight points and five rebounds and felt like an integral part of the team. Midway through the season, when Jack Sikma, our all-star center, injured his ankle, I even got a chance to start nine games and averaged 15 points and 10 rebounds during that stretch, further demonstrating my value to the team.

When Jack returned, I resumed my sixth-man role. Without question, I deserved to be a full-time starter on that team, and Lenny Wilkins acknowledged that on several occasions. He explained that in order for this particular team to succeed, he really needed me to come off the bench.

When I speak to kids at basketball camps I always preach about how important it is to embrace your role, and how every team has somebody who has to sacrifice. I was that guy because Lenny needed me to come off the bench. So I did it. We were winning, and it was the closest team I ever played with in the NBA. I hadn't experienced that type of camaraderie since college, so I really enjoyed that season. The only negative is that our 12-0 start, which eventually became 34-13, only gave us a game-and-a-half lead over the Los Angeles Lakers. As soon as we slipped up, Earvin and his gang cruised by us on their way to the NBA Finals.

# NOT THE CLIPPERS

During the course of my fourth season, I had been thinking that if I ever was going to be traded again, I didn't want it to be to the Utah Jazz or the San Diego Clippers. San Diego's a wonderful city with great weather, but it did not have a good basketball team and I did not want to go through that again. I'd rather come off the bench in Seattle and be part of a good sound team that wins. Of course, during the off-season, I was traded to the Clippers, who were looking to acquire Sonics center James Donaldson. Seattle wanted Tom Chambers in exchange, and when the dust settled I was included, while Seattle also got Al Wood.

It was miserable for a couple of reasons. We weren't winning, and by then my dad, who had quit smoking 10 years earlier, was diagnosed with lung cancer and was in Detroit fighting for his life. He was constantly on my mind, and I had a hard time reconciling my priorities of job and family. My dad would tell me, "Look Greg, you've got a job to do and don't worry about me. Your mom and I are getting older, so things like this can happen." He was trying to comfort me, but he and my mom were in their mid-40s, so that was tough to buy.

## SAYING GOOD-BYE TO WALTER KELSER

My dad survived only 16 months after he was diagnosed with lung cancer. It was difficult being away from home, especially since my dad had always been a pillar of strength and model of health. Every time I went home during the course of the season, I wondered if it was going to be the last time I'd see him alive.

The Clippers had a pretty good roster that included Bill Walton, Terry Cummings, Ricky Pierce, Craig Hodges, Billy McKinney, and the late Derrick Smith who was an up-and-coming star. We won 30 games, and I averaged 11 points and five rebounds as a sixth man, but nothing really mattered as far as basketball was concerned. I tried my best to be professional and worked as hard as I possibly could, but I can't tell you how difficult it was to go to practice and keep my mind on a game when I knew my dad was 2,000 miles away dying. When the Clippers did not make the playoffs, I was able to return home in April and spend a lot of time with my dad. He passed away on July 30, 1984.

I spent three and a half up-and-down months with my dad, and he was in and out of the hospital, but I was with him till the end. When he passed away, I had no regrets, because nothing more needed to be said. He loved me and knew I loved him. He was a major influence in my life. I didn't dwell on the fact that he was just 48 years old. I said to myself that I had been blessed to have my dad for 26 years, and that's 26 more than some kids get. It's been 22 years since he's been gone, and not a day passes without me thinking about him.

## CLOSING DOWN A BASKETBALL CAREER

The 1983-84 season was my last full year in the NBA. I sat out most of the following season trying to get a decent contract because the

Clippers hadn't offered one. I thought that I was going to sign with the Los Angeles Lakers, and be reunited with Earvin Johnson, because Jamaal Wilkes was out with a severe knee injury. I kept myself in shape while sitting out, but at that particular time the NBA had a right-of-first-refusal provision, and the Clippers, who by then moved to Los Angeles, still owned my rights even though I was a free agent. If the Lakers had signed me, then the Clippers would have been due compensation and they made it clear they wanted a No. 1 pick in exchange for my rights. How can you demand a No. 1 pick for a guy you don't even want to sign? They weren't going to let their new cross-town rival get me.

I eventually signed with the Indiana Pacers and played the last 10 games of the season. The NBA and its owners took a firm stance on free agency that year, and nobody was moving. A lot of players sat out, and their careers suffered, mine included. That's how my career came to an end. I thought about going to a training camp the following year to try to make a team that way. I even considered a few good offers to play overseas as a way of facilitating a return to the NBA, but I was nearly 28 years old, and my knee still required medication.

So I weighed things out. I had done a good job of investing my money, so I felt at ease with my decision to move on to the next chapter in my life. Maybe I would have kept chasing the ball if my knee had been close to 100 percent, but if that had been the case I wouldn't have had to chase anything. I always felt in my heart that if I had stayed as healthy in the NBA as I did at Michigan State, where I missed only one game in four years, I not only would I have been an all-star, I eventually would have found my way to a championship. I firmly believe this, because I had already made significant strides. I had gone from 14 points a game as a rookie to 22 points per game in the early part of my second year, and nobody could stop me. I could score on anybody. I may not have been a great NBA player in the same sense as Earvin Johnson, but I would have been a very, very good one. There's no doubt in my mind, because it always had been that way. I started at the bottom in high school and became one of the top prep players in the state of Michigan. I started from the bottom at Michigan State and became an All-American and a champion. It definitely would have happened in the NBA as well.

# 13

# MAKING IT AS A BROADCASTER

## PLANNING FOR LIFE AFTER BASKETBALL

Even though my dream of becoming a professional athlete was realized, my parents often reminded me that I would not be able to play forever, and I should prepare for the day when the jump shots would no longer fall. I had always felt certain I could make a comfortable transition from hoops to something else, but early in my pro career I wasn't really sure which direction I would look. In college, I thought about becoming a criminal defense attorney, but my interests changed once I was in the NBA.

## A FORTUITOUS MEETING

During our NCAA Tournament run in 1979, I met a gentleman who would play a major role in my life. His name is Charlie Neal. I knew him as a sportscaster for Channel 2 in Detroit, but we had never been formally introduced. I made his acquaintance for the first time in Murfreesboro, Tennessee, after our victory over Lamar. Charlie was wearing a very nice suit, and I noticed he had at least a dozen silver bangle bracelets on his right wrist. They really caught my eye, and I asked him to give me a couple. He said, "If you guys win the tournament, I'll let you select three of your choice." He probably felt safe in making that offer, because we were still four wins away from a title. My next opportunity to speak with Charlie came three months after we beat Indiana State for the national championship, and true to his word, he allowed me to select three of his bracelets.

From that chance encounter, Charlie became my close friend and mentor. During my NBA off-seasons, I often accompanied him to work and got an inside look at the world of broadcasting. Charlie and I would watch playoff games on television with the volume turned down, and we would provide the commentary. That proved to be incredibly valuable, because it put me in touch with my talent while allowing me to find a comfort level, develop a style, and build confidence. It was not unlike the days when Terry Furlow would say, "C'mon young fella, let's work." Charlie had a lot of patience and seemed to enjoy being a role model for a young fella. It was during these mock broadcasts that I realized what I wanted to do after basketball.

# GOING ON THE AIR

In 1982, Charlie departed Channel 2 and became the sports director for Black Entertainment Television (BET) in Washington, D.C. Even though I was playing professional basketball on the West Coast, we talked often. When I did not return to the NBA for the 1985-86 season, Charlie presented me with an opportunity to join him as the analyst for BET's coverage of Historically Black College basketball. That's really how it all began. It all came so naturally. The only difference was that the broadcasts were for real.

My first game for BET featured Southern University at Alcorn State in Lorman, Mississippi. Part of my assignment included interviewing both head coaches. I was extremely nervous because I had never done anything like that before, but Bob Hopkins of Southern and Alcorn's David Whitney could not have been more accommodating or patient with me. For the record, Alcorn won a thrilling game, and I was on my way.

Charlie was instrumental in helping me identify the direction I wanted to take and providing me with my first on-air opportunity. Charlie and I remain very close. He's like a brother to me.

# ALPHABET SOUP

When I look back at the people who were there to aid my transition from professional basketball to broadcasting, I certainly can't forget Bob Page, a Michigan State alum who was also working in sports in Detroit television in the '80s. Bob made a call on my behalf to the executive producer of Pro-Am Sports System (PASS), which was later acquired by Fox Sports Net (FSN), and that led to my first Big Ten assignment.

I made my "second" conference debut in East Lansing with the one of the great games in Spartan lore—MSU versus Michigan; Spartan guard Scott Skiles versus UM's Antoine "The Judge" Joubert. That night, Skiles scored 40 points in 39 minutes to Joubert's 12 in 37 minutes. The game was a 91–79 Spartan rout. Skiles also uttered one of the most unforgettable lines in MSU sports history when he rebuffed Joubert's prediction of a Wolverine victory in the rematch: "Not unless you lose 20 pounds, fat boy."

Twenty years later, I'm immersed in my career as a sports broadcaster and loving it. I have worked more than 1,200 games—from the Michigan high school state basketball championships, to the NCAA men's and women's tournaments, to the WNBA and the NBA playoffs and finals. I've worked for BET, PASS, ESPN, Raycom Sports, CBS, and FSN. I recently completed my ninth season with Fox Sports Net-Detroit and its coverage of Detroit Pistons basketball, and my 12th year with ESPN-Regional's coverage of Big Ten basketball. It has also been my advantage to have shared the broadcast table with some truly solid play-by-play talent. Guys like Charlie Neal, Fred McLeod, George Blaha, Matt Shepard, and Wayne Larrivee to name just a few have helped to make the games that we have covered most enjoyable.

# COOKING UP A LIFE LESSON IN HOME ECONOMICS

There is one more important person I often think about when acknowledging those who played a key role in my second professional career. When I was a student at Detroit Henry Ford High School, someone told me, "You should take home economics because they cook

When I was in college I contemplated becoming a defense attorney but caught the bug to be a broadcaster when I was in the NBA. This profession keeps me plugged into the sport I love and which has done so much for me.
*Photo courtesy of Steve Grinczel*

in class, and you get to eat what you make." I had an opening in my schedule for an elective, so I signed up for home ec. Lenore Davis was a great teacher, and she taught me more than just how to bake cookies.

I didn't realize the importance of it at the time, but she took it upon herself to encourage me to always present myself in a certain positive way while being interviewed. She used to say, "Now Greg, you're going to play college basketball at Michigan State, and if they ever choose to interview you after a game, I don't want to hear you on the television using improper grammar and not being sure of yourself." She'd go on to say, "It saddens me when I see young men, athletes in particular, who can't speak properly in front of a camera."

Whenever I was interviewed during my college career, her words were always there in the back of my mind. How could either of us have known her message, which seemed so innocent at the time, would prove to be so important in my career some 31 years after it was delivered? I also do a lot of motivational and public speaking, and Mrs. Davis' sage advice continues to serve me well.

# 14

# THE TOM IZZO ERA AT MICHIGAN STATE

## UNQUESTIONABLY, THE RIGHT MAN FOR THE JOB

It's almost a footnote in history that Tom Izzo worked as an assistant coach for 12 years under Jud Heathcote, who raised the program to national prominence. Tom graduated from Northern Michigan, but he has been a Spartan for 24 years and the front man for one of the country's most visible and admired programs. I liked Tom a lot the moment I met him. I don't recall the particulars, but I remember the times. It was in the '80s, I was still in the NBA, and I was back on campus playing in those wonderful summer pick-up games.

Tom's passion for coaching was very evident as he sat in the second or third seat on Coach Heathcote's bench. I felt that he would become a good head coach someday. Boy, was I short in my calculation. He became a coaching giant right there at Michigan State. I remember feeling very good about him taking over after Coach Heathcote's retirement for two reasons: (1) I felt that his youth and effervescent personality would serve him well in recruiting blue-chip athletes; and (2), after a dozen seasons served under Coach Heathcote, no one could argue that he hadn't paid his dues. He had more than earned the opportunity to become MSU's head coach.

# TURBULENT TIMES

Tom's first two seasons were, to say the least, turbulent. Many fans refused to be patient as he tried to implement his philosophy and sought to build his own program. Shawn Respert and Eric Snow, who formed the exceptional backcourt tandem during Coach Heathcote's final season, were now in the NBA. When you lose such talent, there's bound to be a drop-off. Tom's teams hovered around the .500 mark, and after two consecutive NIT appearances detractors were wondering if he was up to the task.

I hosted Tom's weekly television show from 1995 to 1998, so we spent a considerable amount of time discussing the strengths and weaknesses of his teams. It was very clear to me that he took losing extremely hard. Midway through his second year, MSU lost five straight Big Ten games. Each loss was more excruciating than the previous one. We taped the show every Sunday morning at 7:30, and to his credit he would always do his best to be optimistic and upbeat as we dissected another tough loss. I would often offer words of consolation because I could see that he was suffering, but we both knew that the only remedy would be time, patience, and better players. I have always felt that a coach is only as great as his players, and if you don't have the requisite talent, then your success as a coach is going to reflect the skill of the players you have. That's true in any sport. Those early results shouldn't have been an indictment on his coaching ability the way they were for those who wanted Tom out. Jud Heathcote had a 10-17 record his first year. As soon as he got a few new players during his second season, his record went up to 25 wins. Had Coach Heathcote gotten smarter all of the sudden? No, he was the same coach, but he had better players.

In retrospect, I think Tom did a fantastic job of getting those two teams into the postseason and avoiding losing records.

# THE TURNING POINT

I couldn't have been any happier for Tom when his program experienced a major upswing in 1997-98. However, even that was preceded by one more assault from his critics screaming for his head after a horrible December home loss to the University of Detroit that left the Spartans with a 4-3 record. After bouncing Wright State, MSU's next considerable test was at South Florida. The nonbelievers were poised to pounce, but the Spartans surprised many by beating the Bulls by 15 points. If that win was unexpected, what happened in the West Lafayette, Indiana, 10 days later could only be described as an absolute shocker.

Tom had pitted his team against the heavily favored Gene Keady–coached Purdue Boilermakers and beat them decisively, 74–57. That win easily stands up as one of the most important of his career. It served notice that a Tom Izzo–coached team could not only compete, but win. Mackey Arena is a tough place to play, and it showed he had the goods and his team had the talent.

Tom and I began to really enjoy the Sunday-morning tapings, because we didn't have to force positivity any longer; it came easily as the wins continued to accumulate. The Spartans had clinched a share of the Big Ten championship as they competed against Purdue in a rematch during the regular-season finale in East Lansing. Everybody knew a victory would result in the outright title, especially the Spoilermakers.

## CO-RRECTING BILLY PACKER

Watching that MSU-Purdue game for the undisputed Big Ten title on television was gut wrenching, because it went back and forth; each team made one big play after another. Although Michigan State lost in overtime, 99–96, I was not sad, because it was probably one of the best games that I've ever seen. Spartan basketball was truly back.

In an effort to acknowledge and thank the fans while honoring his team at the same time, Tom made the decision to unfurl the Big Ten championship banner prior to tip-off. Our old buddy Billy Packer was broadcasting the game for CBS Sports, and whenever the Spartans would fall behind, he'd have his producer show the banner so he could use the Telestrator to write the prefix "co-" in front of the word "champion." Billy would go on to tell the national television audience that should the Spartans lose they'd have to take the banner down to stitch "co-" on it. Ironically, I had the opportunity to chat with Billy two weeks later in New York, and I reminded him that the banner would not have to be altered, and mentioned that had he only looked at the other Big Ten championship banners hanging in the Breslin Center, he would have seen than none of them had "co-" stitched on them, including the one from 1979. To my knowledge, very few teams put "co-" or "shared" or "tied" on their championship banners.

## SPARTAN FAMILY

Although I didn't play for him, I believe Tom Izzo regards me no differently than any one of his cherished former players. I say that because that's exactly how he has always treated me, so much so that he even included me on his list of recipients for a championship ring commemorating his first two Big Ten titles and the national championship. That's right. I now I have five Michigan State championship rings—the two I received as a player in '78 and '79, and the three presented by my honorary head coach, Tom Izzo.

## SELECT COMPANY

Michigan State is extremely fortunate to have had only three coaches since 1969. Few schools can boast such continuity. I don't know how much longer Tom Izzo will guide the Spartans, but MSU supporters should be thankful for his unwavering belief in himself and his relentless drive to build Michigan State into one of the elite programs in the nation.

Any successful program, regardless of sport, understands the importance of recognizing its history. No one does that better than Tom Izzo. He truly enjoys occasions when past players, regardless of who coached them, stop by to say hello, attend a practice, or take in a game. He makes everyone feel at home and wants you to feel like you're still a part of the team. The 20th and 25th reunion weekends on campus that my 1979 championship group enjoyed were initiated by Tom, and you could not have hoped for a more complete and classier schedule of events. We all hated to leave. I remember him saying, "As long as I'm at Michigan State, this is always your home."

# NO GRIPES

After four consecutive Big Ten championships from 1998 to 2001, four Final Four appearances, and the 2000 NCAA championship, it's absolutely farcical that anyone ever doubted the coaching ability of Tom Izzo. If we could assemble every MSU basketball fan in Spartan Stadium and ask them if they were a doubter during the 1995-96 and 1996-97 season, I'm sure all we would get is "no gripe, no gripe, no gripe."

Seems like I've heard that before.

By turning MSU into an elite program while embracing former players like me, shown at halftime of the 2004 NCAA Tournament game against Nevada, Spartan head coach Tom Izzo has continued to build on what Coach Heathcote started.
*Photo courtesy of Michigan State University*

# 15

# SPARTAN TIES THAT BIND

## THE LATE, GREAT TERRY FURLOW

I didn't make my first visit to Michigan State until two weeks after I signed my letter-of-intent. I made the trip to East Lansing with my mother, father, and brother, Raymond, who was nine years old. It was a chance to see my home for the next four years, but the coaches also used my visit as an opportunity to meet several of my future teammates, including Benny White, Bob Chapman, Edgar Wilson, and of course the incomparable Terry Furlow.

Meeting Terry was important for several reasons. First, he was the unquestioned leader and star of the team. Second, Terry had developed a reputation for being somewhat of a hot head. I made a point of not believing everything I heard about Terry, because I wanted to get to know him and draw my own conclusions. Some of Terry's problems could be traced to the infamous walkout of January 1975, but more recently he had at least two fights including one with a teammate. Outside observers arbitrarily concluded he had a bad attitude.

There was a knock on my hotel door early Saturday morning. I will never forget how I immediately felt in awe of Terry as he stood in the doorway and introduced himself. "Hello, I'm Terry Furlow," he said. Man, there was a presence about him. We went for a ride in his 1973 Mercury Montego—which was a great-looking car and also impressed me to no end—and we stopped for breakfast. We spent time talking about basketball and school. Terry also said that if all the good things he had heard about me were true, I should be able to contribute immediately, and he looked forward to having me as a teammate. That meant a lot to me. In spite of all the negative things I had heard about Terry Furlow, I came away from our meeting with a very favorable opinion of him.

Soon after my freshman season began, Terry taught me the value of work ethic. He'd come early to practice and stay late to work on his game. Even though he was the most talented guy on the roster, he was always the last to leave the gym. He worked longer and harder than anybody, and he made me stay with him.

He called me "Young Fella," and after practice he'd say, "C'mon Young Fella, let's shoot." I'd rebound for him, he'd rebound for me, we'd play one-on-one. I'd say, "Terry, I gotta go. They're going to stop serving food in the dorm at 6:30."

And he'd reply, "Don't worry about it. You'll come eat with me." Then we'd go to his place and his girlfriend would cook dinner for us, or we might stop and eat at a local restaurant. That's the kind of guy he was.

Terry had a great senior year. He averaged 29.4 points overall and 31 in Big Ten games. I won just one game in Purdue's Mackey Arena during my career, and it was because Terry hit a last-second shot to beat the Boilermakers in 1976. It was a 19-footer, and when he shot it I knew it was going in. I expected every shot Terry Furlow took to go in. That's how good he was.

He also was a tough guy and midway through that season I was playing against him in the upstairs gym in Jenison Field House. We got tangled up underneath the basket while jostling for rebound position and he hit me really hard in the chest with his elbow. He was angry and literally laid it to me. I made the snap judgment to give an elbow right back to him just as hard as I could in his chest.

I was fearful of what might happen as a result of my reaction, but I felt it was important to respond whether I got my ass kicked or not. To my surprise, it went no further and we continued playing as though nothing had happened. I always felt like I had earned some respect because if I had backed down and allowed him to get that shot in without any retaliation, he probably would have thought less of me. I stood up to him and that was the only negative exchange we ever had.

I expected every shot I saw the incomparable Terry Furlow take to go in. Terry is the only Spartan to ever score 50 points in a game, and his three-game stretch of 50 against Iowa, 48 against Northwestern, and 42 versus Ohio State in 1976 is nothing short of phenomenal. As intense a competitor and hard a worker as I've ever been around, Terry would have posted even more incredible numbers if the 3-point line had been in effect. I truly believe he deserves to have MSU retire his number.
*Photo courtesy of Michigan State University*

I think that was Terry just being Terry. He had to scrape from a lot of things while growing up in Flint, Michigan. He wasn't highly touted coming out of high school and had to work his way to the top. I really admired Terry and wanted to be like him. He was the one player, at any level, who had the biggest impact on me, because I saw first-hand how hard he worked. I would not have spent the time in the gym had he not twisted my arm. I would have left just like everybody else. But there we were, late into the evening, and it always meant a lot to hear him say, don't worry about food—you'll eat dinner with me.

He is kind of the forgotten man of MSU basketball, and that's really unfortunate. He still holds school records for points in a game (50), scoring average in a season (29.4 in 1975-76) and single-season field goal attempts (653 in 1975-76). He was the first player from Flint to be an NBA first-round draft pick—he was chosen by the Philadelphia 76ers—and he played in three playoffs, each with a different team.

Terry was embarking on his fifth NBA season when he was killed in a tragic car accident in May 1980 outside of Cleveland. My dad called with the shocking news that Terry was dead, and I was severely shaken. I remember feeling frozen and hollow. It seems like people can't recall Terry without bringing up his so-called negative image. However, he was tremendously popular in the NBA, as evidenced by those who attended his funeral. At least 20 NBA players traveled to Flint to pay their last respects. I was a pallbearer with Julius Erving, Earvin Johnson, and Campy Russell.

In my heart, I believe Terry's number should be retired at MSU. Hanging his No. 25 up there with my 32 and Earvin Johnson's 33 would diminish nothing at all. For 19 years, our numbers were the only two that were retired in Spartan basketball history. I always assumed it was due to the national championship on our resumes. Clearly, since 1995, the criteria have changed to include other standout performers such as Scott Skiles, Shawn Respert, Steve Smith, and Johnny Green. Unfortunately for Terry, there were no championships or Final Four appearances, but dismissing his contribution as a solely individual endeavor discredits his significance in Spartan tradition, because every last bit of him was about team. That was evident in the way he embraced an unproven freshman in 1975 and shared his secrets of hard work, not to mention his dinner.

## LOVE IS BLIND

Benny White was another senior who helped facilitate my transition to Michigan State. He was our point guard, and while I have many memories of Benny, the one that truly stands out occurred during our game at Illinois in 1976. It was a nip-and-tuck contest, and early in the second half I took an elbow in the mouth and sustained a large laceration. I was bleeding all over the place and taken to the locker room. After having the gash stitched closed and bandaged, I returned to the game and played a significant part in our victory that day. Afterward, Benny was the first to hug me, and with my lip swollen to three times its normal size, he looked me in the eye and said, "You know I love you, don't you?"

# PILSON WILSON

"Pils" was my nickname for my 1976-77 teammate and good buddy Edgar Wilson. His last name had been misspelled one time with a *P* instead of a *W*, so I began calling him Edgar Pilson, which I eventually shortened to Pils. Edgar could possibly be the best athlete to ever play basketball for Michigan State. As a high schooler in Dowagiac, Michigan, he dominated in practically every sport.

We used to get a kick out of watching Edgar punt basketballs up to the apex of the Jenison Field House. Nobody else could get the ball up to the inverted V in the center of the ceiling.

Coach Heathcote used to say Edgar led the country in deflections, because although he wouldn't come up with the steal in most cases, he could get his hand on the basketball and knock it out of bounds like no one else.

The only game I ever missed as a Spartan was the last one of Edgar's college career. We were playing at Illinois, and I spent the day in a Champaign hospital with an appendicitis attack. I listened to the game on the radio as Edgar fittingly hit an 18-foot jumper at the buzzer to give the Spartans a one-point victory. Those were his final two points for the basketball team, but he wasn't done scoring for Michigan State. As a fifth-year senior, Edgar started at wide receiver and scored two touchdowns for the Spartan football team. Andre Rison, Lorenzo Guess, and Matt Trannon came over from the MSU football team to play basketball, but how many basketball players are tough enough to go play football?

I'll be forever grateful to Edgar, because he always let me borrow his car before I got my own set of wheels.

# THE ENFORCER

Bob Chapman was a super teammate and our enforcer. Nobody screwed around with Bobby C. This guy was built like Adonis, even though he never lifted weights. Because he had toiled during some of

MSU's sparse years, I always wished that he could have been a part of our national title team. Thankfully, he was a vital member of the 1978 Big Ten championship squad. I remember two guys in particular who made the gross miscalculation of thinking they could challenge Bob on the court. He responded by delivering vicious forearm shivers to Michigan's Steve Grote and Detroit's Wilbert McCormick just below each of their chins. Amazingly, he wasn't whistled for either blow, and we only became aware of them while watching game film. We all laughed about it then, and still do whenever we get together.

## LEAPERS OF A FEATHER

For the longest time, I knew of Johnny Green only through the history books and his pictures hanging on the walls inside Jenison Field House. I was well aware that he had led the Spartans to their first Final Four appearance in 1957, and that he was the school's all-time leading rebounder until 1979. I finally crossed paths with him in Seattle at the 1987 NBA All-Star game. It was an honor to meet him, but I think he was equally honored to meet me. We embraced and shared a few stories. I felt an immediate bond form between us even though our careers were separated by nearly 20 seasons. I'm extremely proud to say 27 years later that I am Michigan State's all-time leading rebounder with 1,092 boards over a four-year span, but I tip my hat to "Jumping" Johnny Green, who collected 1,036 rebounds in just three seasons. Thank goodness for freshman eligibility, which was reinstated in 1973.

## DELIVERING THE BLOW FROM WHICH MICHIGAN STILL HASN'T RECOVERED

Scott Skiles was one tough SOB and made such an impression with his grit and his determination as a freshman my dad told me, "That's the guy who's going to break your scoring record." While my dad didn't live to see it, he couldn't have been more prescient, because Scott improved and became more unstoppable each year. My first Big Ten game as a broadcaster was the big Michigan State-Michigan showdown at Jenison Field House in 1986. Scott led the Spartans to a convincing victory with 40 points. Michigan eventually won the Big Ten championship, but the Wolverines lost both games to MSU, primarily because of Scott Skiles. Michigan hasn't finished atop the league standings since. Against Indiana late in Scott's senior year, he dropped me to the No. 2 spot on Michigan State's all-time scoring list. I watched the game on TV and was extremely happy for him. I held the record for seven years—I'm currently hanging on to fourth place behind Shawn Respert, Steve Smith, and Scott—and was pleased to pass the mantle to such a fierce and fiery competitor.

## SKINNY STEVE SMITH

I remember watching Steve Smith play as a freshman and thinking that this really skinny kid might be pretty good some day, but I don't think anyone imagined that he would scale the heights he eventually reached—2,263 points, 25.1 points per game as a senior, Big Ten title, Olympic gold medal, NBA championship. Although I was in my early 30s when Steve's Spartan career began, I played against him in those famous pick-up games back on campus. Dr. Charles Tucker, a former instructor at Michigan State and solid basketball player in his own right, set up and participated in many of those informal games for years. "Tuck," as we all referred to him, recognized Steve's need to play against as much veteran and experienced competition as he could find, and often stacked the competition against him. This wasn't unusual, because when Earvin and I were in school, Tuck was responsible for getting his friends, such as George Gervin, Darryl Dawkins, and Campy Russell, to compete against us.

While playing against Steve, I was surprised at his strength given his lean frame. By the time he was a junior, he had become one of the nation's best players, and in 1990 led Michigan State to its first Big Ten championship since the one we won 11 years earlier. Steve, of course, went on to great success in the NBA, but his legacy is rooted in his generosity. Steve's unprecedented donation of $2.3 million helped MSU build its state-of-the art student-athlete academic center, which has become a model for universities across the nation and is named in honor of his mother, Clara Bell Smith.

# THE FLINTSTONES

In 1995, Antonio Smith, Mateen Cleaves, Morris Peterson, and Charlie Bell all worked at a basketball camp I conducted for young players in Flint, Michigan. Tone, Mateen, Morris, and Charlie were still attending Flint-area high schools and trying to decide their future. Who fathomed at the time that those four would form the nucleus of Michigan State's 2000 national championship team? I paid them $300 each for the week and they were happy to get it. I'm sure their rates have gone up substantially since then.

Antonio was Tom Izzo's first signee and was the heart and soul of his first Big Ten championship team in 1998-99. With 1,016 rebounds, he is the only other Spartan to grab 1,000 in a career along with Johnny Green and me.

Despite not being the greatest shooter, or the greatest ball-handler, or the greatest defender, Mateen's leadership qualities set him apart from the rest. Much like Earvin Johnson, he would will his team to victory when defeat seemed certain. I'm sure before long, the three-time All-American will have his No. 12 raised in MSU's Breslin Center.

Mo-Pete deserved much respect because of the way he overcame adversity throughout his career. First it was his weight, second it was his lack of defensive intensity, third it was a broken wrist, and fourth it was not making the starting lineup. He conquered each obstacle with tremendous heart, and as a junior became the only sixth man to be named first-team All-Big Ten.

Charlie Bell's career can be encapsulated as follows: four Big Ten championships, three Final Fours, and one national championship. Charlie came in as a prolific scorer out of high school and he evolved into a great defensive player and invaluable utility man with a college resume few can rival.

# FIRE & ICE

The two greatest shooters I ever saw play Michigan State were Terry Furlow and Shawn Respert. I mentioned that I expected every shot Terry ever attempted to go in, and the same went for Shawn.

Everything about his jump shot was perfect—the release, the arc, the follow-through—just magnificent.

I recall when Shawn was a junior, he always wanted to take the big shot in the waning moments of tight games. The problem was everyone knew he was going to have the ball in his hands, and they would double and sometimes triple-team him. Invariably, the shot would be a tough one, while perhaps the better decision would have been to pass the ball. After Shawn made his decision to return to MSU for his senior year, which was the right thing to do, we had a conversation about those late-game situations. I explained to him that while he is a great shooter and a terrific scorer, I still believe that an open shot by one of his teammates was a better option than a forced shot from him. I told him to "trust your teammates. They will reward you."

His senior season ranks as one of the school's all-time best. He averaged 25.6 points per game to overtake Steve Smith as MSU's career scoring king. Ironically, Shawn heeded my advice, and during that year Eric Snow delivered a game-winning shot, as did Daimon Bethea and Jon Garavaglia. Shawn, who scored all but three of his 33 points in the second half after spraining his ankle during the win at Michigan, became a better all-around player.

Indiana's Calbert Cheaney is generally recognized as the greatest scorer in Big Ten history with 2,613 points overall to Shawn's 2,531. However, I believe the distinction belongs to Shawn, because Cheaney played in 13 more games and averaged 19.8 points over the course of his career to Shawn's 21.2. Furthermore, Shawn stands alone atop the Big Ten career-scoring list for conference-only play. In a like number of games against comparable competition, Shawn scored 1,545 points to Cheaney's 1,406, which ranks sixth.

Shawn was a lottery pick in 1995, although his stay in the NBA was a very short and uneventful one. For a long time, people believed he simply lacked the talent to be a good professional basketball player. Nearly eight years later we learned that Shawn developed stomach cancer while playing for the Milwaukee Bucks and chose to keep it to himself—he didn't even tell his parents—amid all the negative speculation about his unimpressive production. I wonder if those opinions have changed now that his struggle was made public. Turns out, he was fighting a far more formidable foe than anyone could have imagined, and won. Therefore, he may have just been the toughest guy in the entire league that year.

I have so much respect for Eric Snow because he worked to make himself a good college basketball player after coming out of high school as a power forward and being converted into a point guard by Coach Heathcote. Eric then used the exact same formula for success in the NBA. Eric understood that he was not a great offensive player, and in order to make a sustained impact on his team he needed to be a defensive stopper. I remember Eric telling me about advice he had received from his dad before coming to Michigan State, and that same instruction was repeated prior to his NBA debut. The message was perfect, yet very simple. Eric's dad told him to "work hard and keep your mouth shut." Clearly, Eric took his father's timeless words to heart while using them to realize unbelievable success beyond even his wildest dreams.

# 16

# A MICHIGAN STATE OF MIND

## PLAYING A BIG ROLE IN THE GAME THAT CHANGED THE GAME

Our national championship game against Indiana State remains one of the all-time great watershed events in the history of sports. Notice that I didn't restrict it to just basketball or even college basketball. The anticipation for the duel between Magic and Bird was such compelling theater; the television rating of 24.1—for a 38-percent share of the viewing audience—remains a record. Our game was the tipping point from which the NCAA Tournament became a national phenomenon, and the Final Four the world's greatest single sporting event in the minds of many. Because of our game, "March Madness" is a common term in our language and even non-sports fans know what a bracket-buster is. Our game ushered in the era of multibillion-dollar television contracts and the seemingly non-stop televising of college games from November to April. Would it have been the same if DePaul and Penn had played for the 1979 NCAA title?

Perhaps.

I always believed strongly that if I had not picked up that fourth foul and stayed on the floor, we wouldn't have stopped the flow of our offense, and the lead wouldn't have shrunk from 16 to 6. It would have gone to 26 points, and we would have won in a rout.

Maybe by virtue of the fact it did become more competitive down the stretch is why the game is still remembered for more than Earvin and Bird going at each other. If it had been a 30-point blowout, maybe it wouldn't have been able to command the attention it has for the last 30 years.

If it was indeed the game that changed the sport, I'm honored to have been a part of it. Even today, if the game is mentioned, ultimately Earvin and Larry are the main reason why. But I find that quite often, somewhere my named gets mentioned as well, and to me that's a feat. You never hear of another Indiana State player mentioned, or one from Michigan State for that matter, even though Terry Donnelly had 15 points and didn't miss a field goal, which was critical to our winning the game.

I think all of my teammates get a sense of satisfaction for being in the right place at the right time, of being blessed and afforded that opportunity, and being able to wear a commemorative ring from that event. We were all a big part of it, because *it* wasn't just that game. *It* was every day and every night from the beginning of September all the way to March 26, 1979.

I often wonder if Arkansas had emerged victorious from that regional final versus Indiana State and became our final opponent, would the game have captured the imagination the same way? Would they still have been showing replays of it 10 years later? Would they have done documentaries on it 20 years later? Would they be referring to it on sports shows 25 years later as "The Game That Changed the Game?"

I doubt it.

# WHAT IF?

I used to think all the time about how things would have been different if we had captured the NCAA championship in 1978, the year before we won it all. It used to haunt me, because it would have been nice to have two national titles. You take UCLA out of the mix and there aren't a lot of schools that can boast back-to-back championships—certainly not a lot of players who can say that. Since UCLA's run with ten titles from 1964 to 1975, only Duke has won two in a row, in 1991 and 1992.

I tortured myself for a long, long time and eventually got over it by thinking that one is better than none. I finally realized, when I got to the ripe old age of 35 or so, that it was time to stop worrying about what I didn't get and be thankful for what I've got. That's how I deal with it now. As you grow older, you look at things differently. You look at things that really bothered you, and you laugh at them.

# IT'S NEVER ENOUGH

I mentioned that sometimes what you do is never enough. That's how it was for me throughout my career. While it bothered me back then, it doesn't bother me now, although I'm reminded from time to time that things haven't changed all that much.

I was the first Big Ten player ever to score 2,000 career points and get 1,000 rebounds. Only two have done it since, and both were centers, Herb Williams and Joe Barry Carroll. When I left Michigan State I was the school's all-time leading rebounder and scorer. I'm still the rebounding leader and fourth in scoring.

Even with all of that, I was never named Big Ten Player of the Week. Not one time. In my estimation, I was always being overlooked. I didn't make first-team All-Big Ten until my senior year. Fortunately, I was named All-America that year as well, but it took me four years to be first team in my own conference.

I remember when Michigan State was starting its Sports Hall of Fame, and they were going to bring 30 members into the charter class in 1992. They sent me this big questionnaire asking why I thought I should be in the hall of fame and to list my accomplishments. I felt very awkward doing it, thinking why should I have to rehash my career and try to convince them that I am worthy? Wasn't it right there for all to see? At that point, we still had only one national championship of which I was a critical part. Until Chris Hill joined me in 2004, I was the school's only first-team basketball Academic All-American.

When the selection committee didn't include me in that charter group, while electing to induct softball players, track athletes, and swimmers, I said to myself, "I won't ever fill one of those out again. If I've got to campaign for this, then I don't want it." I was thrilled when I was finally inducted in 1996, but the delay served as another reminder that sometimes what I did was never enough.

# BIG TEN HIGH-WATER MARK

I wanted to play in the Big Ten because it was a strong and highly regarded basketball conference. I competed from 1975 to '79, a four-year stretch that, in my opinion, was the best in the league's history. Indiana defeated Michigan for the '76 national title and finished undefeated at 32-0. We, of course, won it all in '79. The Big Ten provided the NBA with the overall No. 1 pick in '77 with Indiana's Kent Benson, in '78 with Mychal Thompson of Minnesota, and '79 with Earvin Johnson. And Hoosier small forward Scott May was the No. 2 pick in '76.

# A BOX OF STUFF

I gave every trophy I ever won away almost immediately after I got it. They just didn't mean a lot to me. I still have the gold medal we won in Brazil, my championship rings, and the two watches we got for winning the national title. I have the net from the title game against Indiana State. It's with the ball I used in the win over Michigan to break the MSU scoring record. I also have the ball from the win over Notre Dame that put us in the Final Four.

I've never been big on stuff like that. What I have and cherish are the memories, friendships, and associations, which are unbelievable. I hope I'll always have them close at hand.

# THANK YOU, AL MCGUIRE

When I first watched a rebroadcast of our game versus Indiana State and Larry Bird, I discovered that the late Al McGuire, who was an NBC analyst with Billy Packer and Dick Enberg, showered me with some pretty flattering accolades. While I was sitting out for eight minutes and we were losing our 16-point lead, he said, "I don't want to disappoint the Magic fans, but Greg Kelser means everything to this team." That was nice because while I loved having Earvin as my teammate, I always wanted to be acknowledged for my own individual ability and greatness.

I believed I could fly, and I flew to heights I surely imagined.
*Photo courtesy of Michigan State University*

To be able to pull that off to whatever extent I did on our team while winning a national championship was always gratifying to me. I think my worth and value were clearly demonstrated when I was sitting on the bench and our lead fell from 16 to 6. We're still talking about a game that involved two of the greatest players ever, however, and for me to emerge as a difference-maker makes me feel pretty good.

Al McGuire said, "the third man in the ring made the difference, and that was Greg Kelser." I feel that had I been Larry Bird's teammate that night instead of Earvin Johnson's, Indiana State would have won the 1979 national championship.